The Lions of
Living Free

Susan Hampshire and Nigel Davenport
in the film 'Living Free'

Jack Couffer

The
Lions of
Living
Free

E. P. DUTTON & CO., INC.
NEW YORK   1972

Published simultaneously in Canada by Clarke, Irwin & Company
Limited, Toronto and Vancouver

SBN: 0-525-14648-2
Library of Congress Catalog Card Number: 72-075015

No one alone can accomplish the multitude of interrelated jobs involved in the making of a feature motion picture. It is a co-operative effort and in the final analysis, in the same way that a chain is not stronger than its weakest link, or a machine is only as effective as its smallest part, so a film production depends upon each member of the team.

It is in this spirit that I wish to thank every one of the people who worked so hard in making *Living Free*. Their names will be found in alphabetical order at the end of the book.

JACK COUFFER

Contents

Illustrations

All photographs by Jack Couffer except those
marked as follows:

  *by A. Ballard, Columbia Pictures Corporation
  †by Columbia Pictures Corporation
  **by W. Suschitzky

The author would like to thank the above for permission
to reproduce their photographs.

Preface

Twelve years ago in Kenya, East Africa, a Game Warden's wife named Joy Adamson wrote a story about a remarkable true relationship between herself, her husband, and a group of lions, the principal one of which was named Elsa. The book became an immediate best-seller, and was followed by two more, *Living Free* and *Forever Free*, which chronicled the further adventures of the Adamsons and their relationship with the family of cubs to which Elsa had given birth in the wild.

A film version of *Born Free* was also a smashing success, and it became our hope to translate the next book in the series into an equally effective film.

Several years had passed since the making of *Born Free*, and many of the people who had been associated with its production were not available at the time when Columbia Pictures, and the producers of the original motion picture, Carl Foreman and Paul Radin, decided to film its successor. To my great good fortune, my background as a director of films with animal and natural history backgrounds seemed to qualify me to direct the new film.

Bill Travers and Virginia McKenna, who had played the parts of George and Joy Adamson in *Born Free*, were not available, and we selected two of England's finest artists to carry on the roles. Susan Hampshire, who had just risen to award-winning eminence through her stunning performances on television, and Nigel Davenport, a fine actor with a brilliant record of success, happily accepted the parts. Each of them had been to Africa on previous occasions. Nigel's wife had been born in Kenya, and she still had family living there. As a girl Susan had taken a pilgrimage all alone to visit the famous humanitarian Dr Albert Schweitzer at his remote jungle hospital.

Our production manager, Eva Monley, had grown up in Kenya and had skilfully learned her business while working on most of the important films that have been made in Africa. How odd it is now to think back to that time when Paul Radin and I were considering her employment and wondering if a woman so slight and pretty could handle a job so tough and demanding. If it weren't for her capability, with her appropriately applied sternness or natural tact, we would probably be there yet, bumbling our way through the pains that so often accompany a badly administered film company.

When I accepted the assignment to direct the film I had never been to Africa. Now, after having spent a year in Kenya, I feel like an old resident. There is an infectious magic to East Africa, particularly contagious to a naturalist such as myself, and perhaps the four hundred year old Zanzibar proverb, 'He who sips honey doesn't fail to return to the hive', is really true. It must be so, because I am writing now, after having been months away in England and America, at a makeshift desk made of stacked cartons and safari trunks, under green canvas sheltering me from the equatorial sun, in the Kenya I have come to love.

The making of the motion picture, about which this book is written, seems long ago and the many great controversies and grave arguments regarding the finishing phases of film-making have come and gone. But those conflicts here under the green-barked fever trees have become as insignificant as the dust motes in the blue African sky. The important thing for me about the making of this film was the joy of filming it. And that is what this book is about.

JACK COUFFER

Kenya, East Africa, 1971

1 First Lions

I began to learn about lions the first day I arrived in East Africa. Just beyond the city limits of Nairobi a fence ten feet high runs for twenty miles across the plains. It is not a complete enclosure, only a dog-legged barrier which separates an ancient wild remnant of prehistoric Africa from the young skyscrapers and thronging motorways of the largest city in Kenya. Beyond the fence to the south low rolling hills run uninterrupted for a hundred miles and more, to Tanzania and past the rocky slopes of Kilimanjaro. A game reserve, Nairobi National Park it is called, lies in a narrow strip between the fence and the Athi River. People in ever-increasing numbers dot the southern plains with wattle huts, and rings of stacked thorn branches circle barely productive fields. To reach the refuge, wild animals that for millennia grazed freely, now must thread their ways through herds of cattle and goats that crush the grass and trample the soil to sterile dust. But still the wild herds come and go, in to and out of the south: the zebra and kongoni, the Tommies and wildebeest, Grant's gazelle and impala – and only a thin mesh fence keeps them off the sidewalks of Nairobi.

And with the herds come lions.

The way to find lions in Nairobi National Park is to drive one's car onto a high point of land and to search the surrounding countryside through binoculars. When you have spotted a circle of automobiles parked on the plains you have found your lions.

We drove through the grass between the road and a huddle of cars, bounced across an aardvark hole, and came to rest. A warden in a Land-Rover was talking to the driver of a parked car. I overheard him say that there were six lions in the pride, but to me the circle ringed by closely parked cars looked quite empty. The lions had evidently finished off last night's kill and were lying asleep in the tall grass. Then there was a slight movement. A tawny paw rose out of the grass, stretched lazily and flexed its claws, and I saw the outline of a yellow head blending perfectly with the dry yellow surroundings. The lioness opened one eye, stared sleepily toward us and closed her eye again. She hadn't even troubled to lift her head. Automobiles were scorned by the lions. It was as if they didn't exist, or as if they were only varicoloured boulders jutting from the plains. Other cars came along, engines started (revving louder than was necessary, I thought), horns tooted (too frequently to be accidental), gears crashed, people talked. But the lions didn't move. They couldn't have cared less.

These were the first wild lions I had ever seen – but they didn't seem to me to be very wild, and I really couldn't see them at all well.

We sat for an hour waiting. Nothing happened. Occasionally we observed some tawny fur between the grass, heard the sound of an unseen yawn. Clouds rolled up from below the horizon down Mombasa way and slid across the sun. We ate our sandwiches and drank our beer – and waited another hour. The hot afternoon changed to cool evening.

Then quite suddenly he was there, as if he had materialized out of his surroundings. He stood in regal pose, a full-grown African lion, not quite as I had visualized he would be, surrounded as he was by automobiles, but magnificent all the same. He strode a few paces through the grass, completely aloof to the whispered voices of awe, the clickings of twenty camera shutters and the whirr of super-eight cinematography. Then with a tremendous sigh, he flopped down again into the grass. I could see him now, lying there, head up, alert. The lioness and her half-grown cubs stirred, began to grow restless in the cooling air, prepared for the evening hunt.

The lion seemed to be staring at me – at least I fancied that he was – or was it at something on the plain far beyond the car, perhaps at a distant gazelle moving against the sunset clouds? I had the strange feeling that I could step outside the car in perfect safety, mix with these great beasts and stroke them, so near they were and so indifferent to our presence. Consciously I restrained myself from the impulse. I forced myself to realize that this was truly a wild lion and not a captive in a game park – a savage beast readying himself for the age-old hunt, to kill wild game in a wild land that was really only superficially intruded upon by our knot of little cars.

The lion yawned, and the glimpse into that gaping maw brought an exclamation of appreciation from everyone in the encircling cars, a combined gasp and chorus of awe: 'Ohhh!' His teeth were fantastically large; yellowed fangs, heavy but sharp. There was an impressive feeling of strength as well as of size, and it was not at all difficult to imagine those huge tusks tearing through the armour hide and snapping the neck of a charging buffalo. Then the great jaws shut, and the lion grunted. It had been a mightily impressive demonstration.

In that moment I understood what it was about the African lion that since my boyhood had fascinated me, and I realized that my childish imagination had been unequivocally true. The lion really *was* the ultimate symbol for the king of the wild, the romantic beast of the hunt, the last living remnant from ages past when man and animal shared more common urges. As he stood there in the sunset fanciful words came to my mind, words such as fang and claw, danger, indifference, unafraid, killer, regal. Those searching eyes set in that yellow face against the great black mane were truly splendid, and I fancied that they continued to pry into mine. I studied those eyes, and I saw in them something far more practical than mere romantic words. The lion, I realized, is an ideal subject for filming. In addition to all those singular poetic qualities that attracted me so personally to him, he had the capacity to reveal himself completely in his expressions. This was an important asset from a film maker's point of view. One could look into that great beast's face and understand his thoughts as clearly as if he spoke the English tongue.

Expressiveness is an essential quality for an animal who is to play in films and who cannot, of course, speak the dialogue. Through the simple language of facial expression, of bodily carriage, tension, and movement, the lion can say to man: 'I am interested', 'I am afraid', 'I am happy, angry, bored, sad, hungry,' and he has countless other more subtle variations of communication. He can say what he has to say with a clarity so indelible that it is understood intuitively by any human, no matter how out of tune with the animal world the man may be, and the lion can say it in a way that can be positively recorded by the camera.

The foolish urge to step out of the safety of my car and to mix with these great beasts had passed, but the lion's eyes continued to transfix me – and I knew at once why I was here.

2 Royal Lions

We had thought we might find the tame lions we needed for our film in Africa – perhaps as pets on lonely farms or at some remote game warden's post. A few years ago, one would have found such docile, captive lions. But the countries of Kenya, Uganda, and Tanzania have become increasingly aware of the economic importance of their wild animals (organized hunting and tourists who come to see the wildlife are great sources of income) and strict laws to protect the animals are now rigidly enforced. It is illegal to keep wild animals without special permits and these are not easily granted.

Our lion requirements were specific. Now that we had arrived in Africa, we realized for the first time how difficult they would be to meet.

The film story was to begin at the time that Elsa's three small cubs had to face the world on their own. Elsa was the lion cub brought up by George and Joy Adamson, made famous by the film and book *Born Free*, and then returned to the wild. We were to follow the cubs' lives on film, recording their adventures until they had grown to be nearly mature lions, by which time their mother, Elsa, had died. During their early life they roamed as wild, hungry orphans, attacking domestic goats, until the authorities ordered the Adamsons either to destroy them or relocate them. With much difficulty the cubs were finally trapped by the Adamsons and transported to that paradise for lions, and for all wild animals: Serengeti National Park.

During all of this time in the cubs' lives, the Adamsons were either looking after the cubs' welfare, trying to find them in the

vast African bush, or attempting to capture the trio in order to
transport them to more suitable territory. George and Joy
Adamson did this, of course, without taming the lions, for they
had decided never to make the cubs into pets as they had Elsa,
but to let them grow up wild from the very beginning.

This was what George and Joy Adamson had accomplished in
real life, but for us to film the cubs in the re-creation of their true
story we would need absolute control over the cast of lions who
were taking their parts. We would use no fences, which would
have been very limiting to the scope of photography, yet for the
lions' own good, as well as for our own, we had to know where
the cubs were at all times. A lion cub, wandering around on his
own in the African bush, can get into some remarkable troubles
– exactly as the Adamsons had learned before us and as we were
eventually to discover.

Because in the film story we were to see the cubs actually
grow up before our eyes and because it would not be practical
from the point of production time for us to follow the growth of
the same three cubs, we would need several groups of cubs of
varying ages to represent the three at different times in their
young lives. We therefore needed a trio of small cubs, one of
middle-sized cubs and one of large cubs. In addition, we would
have to take a few scenes of new-borns and of course we must
see Elsa and her mate, the wild father, as adult lions.

Not only did we require lions of these various age groups but
– because of the vastly different personalities and natures of
individual lions – we would require doubles and animals able to
perform a variety of specific tasks. And then, to make this all
more confusing and difficult, because of the many months we
would be in production and because we should not necessarily be
filming chronologically and because lion cubs grow fast, we
would need new groups from time to time to fill vacancies left
by our smallest trios as they grew up into the middle-sized class.

We calculated that our eventual requirements would be for

approximately twenty-five lions. We were not far out. Eventually over thirty performed before our cameras.

Our producer, Paul Radin, who had also produced *Born Free*, remembered that he had obtained lion cubs for that film from the Emperor Haile Selassie of Ethiopia who is proud of his exalted position as The Lion of Judah and keeps a small menagerie of State Lions on the palace grounds as well as a few in the city for public exhibition. Paul flew to Addis Ababa and returned in a few days with the startling news that a magnificent lioness had given birth to a litter of cubs at the very moment of his arrival. He had actually watched the arrival of two of our future stars, and another litter of three had been born only a few days before. Even now, five new-born cubs were flying to us from Ethiopia.

Soon we had lions, but no place to put them. We couldn't look after them in our Nairobi hotel rooms.

Raising five lion cubs is more than a full time job. Formula must be carefully prepared and fed from baby bottles four times a day and twice during the night. They must be exercised; the temperature of their surroundings must be carefully regulated; they must be cleaned, medicated and tended as carefully as a human baby. And each cub, in order that it should grow up to be tame, must be handled, stroked and cuddled every day so that its association with people would be one of affection and pleasure. Our lion handlers, Hubert Wells and Cheryl Shawver, were waiting in California until we obtained lions, but these five cubs were already on their way to us and our handlers had other commitments to fulfil before they would be able to join us.

We called on Marchesa Sieuwke Bisleti at a grand house on a 56,000 acre farm fifty miles north of Nairobi. Sieuwke Bisleti, a Frieslander, grew up in Indonesia and was married to an Italian Marchese. Her two lions, Sheeba and Shaibu, with three of their cubs, had played the parts of Elsa and her mate and cubs at the end of the film *Born Free*.

Marchesa Bisleti kept the lions, along with a considerable

turn-over of other wild animals, because she enjoyed them and wanted to help them. The section of the farm surrounding her house was both animal orphanage and hospital. She had a reputation for dealing with injured animals, abandoned fawns, and orphaned cubs. Her leopards were the offspring of a pair that were trapped rather than shot after they had taken to killing sheep on the farm. She returned many of the animals to the bush after they were healed. Some varieties, unlike lions which require training to cope with the wilderness, were instinctively able to look after themselves when they reached maturity, and these she invariably turned free.

The first lion Sieuwke raised was brought to her thirteen years ago by Major Temple-Boreham, chief game warden in the Narok area of central Kenya. He had seen vultures flying and expecting to find dead game killed by poachers, went to investigate. He found three tiny lion cubs, two dead and one still just alive. The game warden was acquainted with the cubs' mother, a lioness whom he had once saved from death after she had been mauled in a fight and could not move. He had brought her food and water every day until she had recovered. The lioness never forgot, and remembering the sound of Temple-Boreham's Land-Rover, she always came to say 'hello'. But apparently the lioness did not have enough milk to raise these cubs and had abandoned them. Temple-Boreham brought the surviving cub to Sieuwke.

When Sheeba, as Sieuwke named the cub, was a year old, the Marchesa acquired a three-week-old male cub which she named Shaibu. Shaibu grew up with Sheeba, and with seven dogs, two leopards, and a cheetah. Later, when game laws became more strict, because they had been in her care for such a long time, Sieuwke was allowed by the Kenya Game Department to keep the lions.

Over the years, this magnificent pair had produced thirty-seven cubs, and Sieuwke had raised them all by hand. Some had been sent to America to stock the Lion Country Safari parks in Florida and California – indeed some of the kin from these lions eventually returned to Africa to perform in our film. Others of the Marchesa's cubs had been successfully taught to live in the wild, and were part of the pride Joy and George Adamson had freed at Meru in north central Kenya.

Obviously, Marchesa Sieuwke Bisleti had the experience we required, and since our cubs were Royal Lions, wasn't it fitting that they should be looked after by a member of the nobility? Fortunately, the Marchesa agreed and joined our staff as lion trainer-cum-mum.

Sieuwke has the admirable habit of keeping a detailed record, and she has allowed me to quote from it regarding her first experiences with our five cubs which she took over the moment they arrived from Addis Ababa.

The Ethiopians came on August 7th, 1970, and I went to the airport to get them with Monty Ruben [a great friend to all of us on the production, and the most helpful, hospitable and knowledgeable expert regarding his native Kenya]. They were ugly and at the same time adorable. The ugliest were the two smallest who were about a week of age. The three others were twelve days old. As soon as they were cleared by the Health Department and Customs I hurried them home.

The smallest male started drinking milk the first day. He was a greedy little cub, knew what he wanted, and went for it literally with claw and fang. If he was at all dissatisfied, he let me know it in no uncertain terms, and my hands and arms were soon covered with bites and scratches, Band-Aids, and mercurochrome.

In the beginning they all slept in my bed, and at 3.00 a.m., every morning, one greedy little fellow made his way determinedly to my face, bit my nose, and demanded food. I called him The Menace, and naturally his name stuck and eventually became Dennis the Menace.

His little sister was a sweet, timid, little creature and got the name of Dawn at the request of a friend of mine. Judy, very beautiful, full of dignity, and rather aloof, was called after Margaret Burke's daughter, a little girl to whom the cubs seemed like soft toy animals come to life. Francis seemed stupid, stubborn, and very lovable. Why Homerus was called Homerus by my friend Fosca Terranova, I still don't know. He was the biggest and the darkest of the lot, slow in movement, greedy, very shy, and very sweet.

After I had had the cubs for about a month, I bought an old used baby crib. The thought of five lion cubs in bed with me when they were a few weeks old was a little too much, even for me. As it happened, they had to go into the cot sooner than intended because of the nosebiting habit of Dennis the Menace. Even then he was a trouble, always hanging with his head outside through the slats and yelling like mad.

Also before I moved them to the crib, my bed had become a little too wet during the night. It would have been all right if there had been just one or two cubs as was most often the case with Sheeba's litters. Usually I had managed to catch them in time to race outside and let them do what they had to do. But five! Impossible! And even when I thought I had protected myself with a huge sheet of plastic they always succeeded in finding a place where there was none. Cushions, incidentally, were a favourite target.

By August 14th, four cubs were drinking beautifully. The small ones started first, followed by Judy and then Homerus.

Francis, however, was another matter. On August 21st, two weeks after he had arrived, he had not had a single decent meal. I had forced a few mouthfuls of milk down him, but only enough to keep him barely alive. He looked pathetic. His head was huge, and his body seemed to wither, getting smaller and smaller every day. I took him to my friend Heather Campbell, who is a retired veterinary surgeon, and together we nursed him for five days. She could find nothing wrong with him, and we presumed that it was something psychological. Perhaps the airplane trip had been to much for him and he had assumed the defence of full retreat. It took almost more patience than I possessed to stay with it. But finally, on August 22nd, I entered into my logbook: 'Francis eats well for the first time. But he has a hell of a temper!'

From the day Francis started eating, he was no trouble. He got his reputation for being stupid and stubborn during his fasting period, and this was not really fair, for he was not stubborn, certainly not stupid, and very sweet! Eventually, when he had recovered completely, he became a part of one of the trios that appeared in the film. He was the *only* lion to get applause from the film crew after performing a difficult scene. He became the biggest of the five and the easiest to handle. From the most troublesome cub, he grew to be the easiest and most affectionate of the Ethiopian lions.

Although all the cubs were accustomed to people, and I mean not only me, but lots of other people, and were handled by everybody, three of them were very timid. I called these my 'spooky' lions. All cubs get spooky between two months and eight months of age, but some more so than others. Homerus was just timid-spooky. Even Dawn, who had not been afraid of anything, became spooky; and Judy was just aloof-spooky.

The attitude of cubs toward the one who raises them never changes, and they are always trusting and affectionate to that person, but their behaviour toward strangers or toward unfamiliar situations can become distrustful. Not one of the five ever changed in his affection for me, and each one would have been the same with anybody else who might have reared him.

We used to have tremendous adventures. Chasing cattle was one of our games. I often sat on the wall that surrounded the house to watch them. Dawn would hide behind a little bush down in the meadow. Dennis would lie flat as a pancake behind about three blades of grass, thinking he was invisible, and Judy would be in her favourite lurking place behind a fallen log. Francis usually showed himself in full view of the cows, perhaps to hold their attention. Poor Homerus wanted so much to be a part of everything, but he was over-cautious and therefore always too late and got left out. He had a beautiful face with big, brown, rather sad-looking eyes.

Finally Judy would charge and the cattle would stampede with the other lions in hot pursuit behind. Then suddenly, as if on some unheard command, all the cows would turn round and become the pursuers, while the lions raced back to where I sat on the wall laughing my head off.

Sometimes we would go on walks together. Our favourite walk was to the river, and I usually picked flowers on the way. The game they seemed to enjoy most of all was to stalk me from behind, then charge and trip me, throwing me flat on my face, my flowers flying everywhere.

I don't like to admit to favourites, but if I did have one, I think it was Judy. She was beautiful, dignified, independent, with lovely stately movements. She was very motherly toward the other four and pulled at them if she seemed to think they were doing something they shouldn't do or something that could be dangerous. She always seemed to be looking to see that they were all there. If Homerus was selfish and only concerned with getting all the food away from his mates at feeding time, Judy was just the opposite and seemed forever to be looking around to see if her family was all right.

The film company eventually arranged to obtain lion cubs from America. It was most gratifying to me, to see the arrival in Africa of the first lions from Florida – for three years ago I had personally taken three of my lionesses, Sirti, Sonja and Sheeba, to Lion Country Safari park in Florida. Now I recognized family characteristics right away – Sheeba's long distinctive muzzle which is typical of lions from Narok – and I believed that two of the cubs, Arusha and Naivasha, were kin to my lions. After checking records with the park, I discovered that they were granddaughters of my Sirti.

*

At first we had resisted the idea of bringing lions to Africa. It seemed ridiculous – like taking coals to Newcastle – but at last it became obvious that this was the only possible solution. Two large wildlife parks in America, one in Florida and the other in California, were owned and operated by the same management. Between them, they had more than two hundred and fifty lions which were producing cubs at the rate of a half-dozen every month.*

There was another, perhaps even greater advantage to the arrangements we eventually made with the Lion Country Safari parks. On previous films I had accumulated numbers of animals

* Since then the number of their parks has been increased to four.

Our home on Crescent Island, Lake Naivasha

Mike with Kamau . . .

... and his playmates

with which I had become emotionally involved and to which I felt strong attachments. When the films were finished I had to face grave problems as to how to find homes for the animals, places where they could live happily and thereby enable me to fulfil my moral and emotional obligations to them. It had often been a tremendously difficult part of the production and one that involved a degree of sadness. By using animals from Lion Country Safari, we entered into an arrangement by which the future of the lions was known in advance. (They would be returned to the place they had come from.) This offered them a reasonable life in which they would be well looked after in a situation that was, for a lion, perhaps the next best thing to being wild. The two Lion Country Safari parks combined extended over a thousand acres which were divided up into lion living spaces varying in size from about five to over twenty acres.

It was a happy coincidence indeed, that some of the lions in our film were grandchildren of Sieuwke's Sheeba and Shaibu, and had gone all the way 'round circle', as it were, from Africa to America, and back home again.

3 Crescent Island

There were several reasons why we chose Lake Naivasha, a shallow lake approximately five miles in diameter in the highlands of the Great Rift Valley in central Kenya, as a base location. Most importantly, it was cool, which would please the lions – a subtle inducement to co-operation. In order to keep to a businesslike schedule of filming, there would be many times when the lions would be required to perform in front of the cameras all day long. In a hot climate, such as that of the lowlands of Kenya, the lions would have refused to work during the hot hours and would simply have lain down in the shade.

There were other aspects which influenced our choice. At the Lake Naivasha Marina Club there were excellent accommodations for our crew, with good restaurant facilities that would keep our London technicians happy, and there was ample land adjacent to the Marina on which to establish the holding areas for our cast of lions. The countryside surrounding the lake was very varied, much of it resembled the Tana River area where the real cubs Jespah, Gopa and Little Elsa had lived, and within a few miles we could film in such differing locations as dry desert scrub, forests of green-barked fever trees, candelabra or euphorbia groves, mountains, plains, jungles, rivers and lakes.

My personal vote for Lake Naivasha (and here I must admit to a bit of selfishness) was because of Crescent Island. The island was the exposed half-circular rim of an ancient volcano and lay but a few hundred yards offshore. An old farmhouse, the only house on the island, was to be my home for the next eight months.

When the lake was at anything but its highest level, there was a narrow causeway allowing a Land-Rover to be driven on to the island. During the few weeks when the water was very high, I would use a skiff with an outboard motor to travel back and forth between my home and the shore. There was a narrow channel through the lily pads and after the first moonless night when my flashlight shone on a hippo who had noisily raised himself beside my boat, the channel became known as 'Hippo Alley'. Once, years ago, the island had been farmed, now it was a bird and wildlife sanctuary protected by the owners of the Marina. Each time I drove across the causeway was an adventure. Waterbirds by the hundreds used it as a resting place and as I motored slowly along they took off ahead of my car, whirled away, and landed behind me. White-headed fish eagles perched on the drowned trees along the shore, and ospreys, pelicans, snake-birds, crakes, cormorants, geese, ducks, coots and kingfishers occupied snags and swam and waded between the lily pads along the way.

The arc of land held a bay of calm, still water, and the island rose steeply on one side, sloping in the opposite direction in gentle grassy hills. The island was rimmed with a border of green-barked fever trees, and the surrounding shores edged the land with a curtain of softly waving papyrus fronds. Lily pads, dotted with blue and purple blossoms, spread across the shallows. There was a continual noise in the air, a muted cackle of bird sounds, knob-headed coots sounding like a faraway pack of dogs, and the occasional harsh croak of a heron. The laugh of fish eagles rang occasionally, and golden-crowned Kavirondo cranes, courting in the field, gracefully weightless dancers, beat the air with their great wings and called their wild song.

Beyond the house, a herd of more than a hundred water-buck grazed each afternoon, and Thompson's gazelles, bush-buck, and dainty puppy-sized antelope called dik-dik scurried ahead of one along the paths.

Guinea fowl in the field made their rattling wheezing calls or fluttered into the trees when a tawny eagle swooped low above them. A troop of vervet monkeys had a regular route around the island, and passed the house each morning exactly at ten. I could have set my watch by the time of their arrival, so punctual were they.

It was a paradise, this island of mine. Was it any wonder that I earned the reputation among the film crew of being something of a hermit?

My wife, Joan, and our son, Mike, were with me during the summer school holiday, and what an adventure it was for a nine-year-old boy. It was a Tom Sawyer's dream of heaven. Early mornings and evenings he spent fishing for bass along the shore, the days were occupied exploring with his friend Ele, a pet eland, or with his other friend Kamau, a Kikuyu boy who brought a herd of milk cows to the island each day for grazing and drove them back to the mainland at sunset. There was complete rapport between those two, and if Kamau at first failed to understand the importance of capturing beasts so familiar to him as black tarantulas and green grass snakes he soon discovered the excitement of the chase and joined Mike with the complete involvement of a dedicated hunter.

Kamau, in his halting English, won my heart in a single brief conversation:

'Did you learn your English in school?'

'Yes.'

'But you are herding now. You don't have time to go to school?'

'No.'

'Will you be going back to school?'

'Of course!' It was an emphatic reply, leaving no room for doubt.

'When?'

'When my father has enough money.'

'I see. . . .' I paused, wishing now that I had not begun.

Kamau, possibly realizing my embarrassment, continued, 'But my father died.'

I am not enough of a psychologist to interpret Kamau's reasoning, but the wishfulness behind that confused statement was incredibly touching.

When Mike left to return to school in the United States, we gave Kamau a responsible job at the lion camp, helping with the feeding and maintenance of the cubs, but I'm afraid it was a valueless apprenticeship. Yet, the boy grew tall in those months, and surely in his association with us he learned something more than how to care for lions. Or did he only awaken to yearn for something more than he could ever have?

Mike was not at Crescent Island when Rosemary and Basher came. Perhaps it was just as well. They were two full-grown ostriches, the most dangerous animals in our company. A scientist and his wife had acquired two ostrich eggs from a nest on the Athi Plains south of Nairobi and had hatched them in their bed. It had been an unusually wet winter and the chicks had been raised in the house. When the researches were finished, the ostriches came to the island sanctuary to repopulate an area where there had been none of their kind for many years.

It soon became evident how Basher got his name. My household helper, Kinua, saw him pluck one of my socks from the clothesline and swallow it (I now learned that an ostrich has an even more curious taste for the bizarre than the omnivorous goat). Kinua raced outside to retrieve the remainder of the wash, stooped down to pick up a pair of fallen shorts, and Basher laid him out on the grass with a right jab of his foot that opened a gash in his scalp and knocked him unconscious.

From that time on, we regarded Basher with great respect. The two ostriches came every morning at dawn and pecked at the window panes of my bedroom (perhaps in a symbolic wish to return to their embryonic past in the warm bed of the scientist's wife). I am an early riser, and I didn't mind this morning call, in fact I rather enjoyed seeing those two stupid faces peering in at me every day at dawn. It gave me a certain feeling of cheer, like awakening to a humorous animated cartoon.

Once, on my way across the front yard to my Land-Rover, I saw Basher loosening up his wings. He began to flap them in that peculiar pedalling motion that always seemed to precede a charge. I made it just in time to the refuge of a pepper tree where I could circle around on the grass, keeping the trunk between us. I was prepared to spend the day there, but at last Kinua heard my shouts and came to the rescue with a flung slipper. He had learned that Basher invariably responded to a slipper or a shoe thrown with power and conviction, and it was certainly the best way to put him to hasty retreat. We wondered what conditioned response triggered this quirk, but the scientist who had raised Basher had apparently fled the country after inflicting him on us, and I was never able to learn more about the trait. Perhaps it had something to do with his having been raised in a bedroom, where shoes and slippers are usually close at hand.

At any rate, it was that unique attribute, and the wide advertising of its effectiveness, that saved Hubert.

Hubert Wells was our head lion handler. One Sunday morning he walked over to visit me and to photograph some birds on Crescent Island.

He was halfway across the field that stretched below my house when Basher spotted him. I saw the big bird start that pedalling with his wings, and I yelled at Hubert, but it was too late. No man on earth can outrun an ostrich, and for Basher it was a downhill sprint. Hubert is no slouch when it comes to picking them up and putting them down, but Basher was clearly closing the gap. I knew that in a few steps I would see one of those powerful legs strike out and Hubert would be down. It was no joke. Ostriches have been known to rip a man wide open with their powerful feet and legs, and I would rather be kicked by a mule.

Then I saw an incredible sight, perhaps the most astonishing feat of spontaneous acrobatics I have ever witnessed. Somehow, still at full run, hopping for an instant on one foot, then back on two and running, almost without breaking stride, but now with his right shoe in his hand, Hubert had accomplished an incredible feat and saved himself. Truly, the man was gifted. He swerved sharply and I heard his voice boom across the field: 'Hah, Basher! – Got you!' and he flung the shoe, catching the unfortunate ostrich full in the chest. Basher stopped dead in his tracks, and as quick as lightning Hubert reloaded from the left foot. He needn't have bothered. He had won the day. Basher was streaking across the field to join Rosemary and perhaps a bit of socks *á la crème* or shorts *au naturel* from my clothesline.

Later on, a young giraffe was found by a farmer nearby caught in a wire fence. He brought it to the island where Kinua fed it milk several times daily from a huge champagne bottle with a rubber tip. Twiga, as the giraffe was named, developed a fast friendship with the two ostriches and the three of them were never far apart.

★

One sequence in the film required a large male lion to play the part of the cubs' father at the time in their lives just before they struck out on their own. The island was an ideal place to house such a potentially dangerous animal. If he escaped from his quarters, we reasoned, he would still be somewhat isolated, and although lions can swim quite readily, he would probably not venture off the island, which had plenty of interesting territory to investigate. What a pleasure it was to have that huge lion near my home, even for the few short weeks we required him for the filming. Every evening, just after sunset, he brought the island to uneasy attention with his roars. The sound carried far across the hills, but there were no wild lions within the range of his voice, so it was a lonely call that went unanswered, proclaiming a territory that no one wanted; it haunted me. The roar of a lion in the African night is one of the most stirring sounds I know, and those weeks when Thunder shared my island were weeks I will never forget.

One night, however, I was startled to awakenness by the sounds of loud roaring from just outside my window. My first thought was that Thunder had escaped from his cage, and I began calculating how I could safely get to my Land-Rover in order to summon the handlers, and how we could get him back into his cage in the darkness. It was a bright moonlight night and I looked out to where the sounds of roars and deep snortings were continuing. Those roars did sound a bit strange, I thought, but in my half-awake condition I didn't realize *how* strange. What I saw was a series of huge black shapes drifting like grounded dirigibles through the darkness. When two of the blimps approached one another the roaring began. Hippos, eight of them, had grazed up out of the papyrus and were mowing the green watered grass in front of my house.

I sat for an hour on the window-sill as the beasts ghosted back and forth through the moonlight. I remembered the book I had leafed through only a few days before, *African Game Trails* by Theodore Roosevelt. It was to this very lake that he had come to hunt for hippo, and where he finally succeeded in shooting a huge bull. Even then they had been shy animals, but now they were doubtless even more timid and secretive. Later I was to discover that there were many hippos living in Lake Naivasha, though they were seldom seen. But any place where there was papyrus (which was nearly everywhere along the shore) one could find their tracks and tunnels they had beaten through the reeds. By day they stay hidden and only on moonlight nights like this could one see them grazing far from the water on the hills of Crescent Island.

4   Safari

The word, safari, had always seemed to me a trite expression left over from the explorations and expeditions of African pre-colonial times. Before I arrived in Kenya, I would have thought it was a word reserved for tourist operators and old-fashioned movies. In fact I soon discovered that Kenyan locals use the word frequently. It means a trip into the wilds. In modern-day East Africa it can mean a flying tour of the game parks using the most luxurious lodges for accommodation, or a trip anywhere in the bush and life under canvas. For us, safari meant five tents, a small staff to run our camp, a few portable lions' cages, assorted four-wheel drive vehicles, lions, trainers, myself, and one small camera that was the fragile fulcrum on which this top-heavy company balanced.

The filming of *Living Free* was divided into two basic phases: what we called the second unit or animal photography unit which consisted principally of the small safari outfit, and the main photography unit which included the stars, a full-sized crew of fifty technicians and all the transport, logistics and support that backs up any other small army.

The two phases were done separately for reasons of both convenience and economy. Several sections of the scenario dealt with the cubs' experiences with other animals, or the script described adventures of the cubs while on their own, away from any contact with people. These sequences could be filmed most effectively with a bare minimum of crew. In animal photography, any unnecessary people, even those with the best of intentions and understanding, cause distraction to the animals, and at times visitors or crew members can unwittingly become disruptive. The mere presence of people is invariably unsettling.

I recall one incident that took place when we were filming *The Incredible Journey*, which was a story about two dogs and a cat travelling through the Canadian wilderness. The scene we were attempting to photograph required considerable attention on the part of a Labrador retriever, one of the trio of animal actors. But at the critical point of action, in every take, he was repeatedly distracted by something from out of camera range, and he looked up and stared with intense fixation in the wrong direction. After we had tried to shoot the scene a dozen times with the same dismally unsuccessful result, one of the handlers unobtrusively circled around behind a small group of onlookers who had been watching from the sidelines. They were important visitors, production executives from the distributing company, and they had been co-operating completely, remaining still and quiet as we had instructed them to do. But again, at exactly the same time in the progression of the scene, the Labrador's head spun around and he stared in the direction of the rooted visitors.

This time, the suspicious animal handler, perhaps a bit carried away at having discovered the culprit at last, grabbed the Board Chairman's wrist where his hand entered his trousers' pocket, held it, and shouted: 'Got him!'

The poor man, while watching the scene unfold, wishing nervously for its successful resolution, had become increasingly tense as the shot approached its climax. And at the same time in each take, when the suspense reached its height, he began, unconsciously, with nervous preoccupation, to finger the coins in his pocket. The tiny sound of coins clinking together in the distance had been inaudible to us, but of course the dog heard it clearly, and the subtle distraction, interesting to his finely tuned ear, threw his performance out perhaps even more emphatically than a shot would have done.

In *Living Free*, in addition to the practical reasons for filming the animal scenes with a small second unit crew, there was the obvious saving of production costs. It would have been wasteful to staff the unit with all the technicians required for full-scale production for the three months we required to photograph only the animals. Susan Hampshire and Nigel Davenport, the two stars of the film, would not be joining us until we had completed the second unit shooting. The dialogue-recording crew, make-up department, costumer, prop men, and all of the other people required to back up the expanded main unit, would be needed only for the main phase of production, that part of the story which dealt with the stars and their relationships with the animals and with each other.

It was for these reasons that we made the film in two sections, unrelated during the actual shooting. Months later, in the London cutting rooms, the two sections would be interwoven into one continuously unfolding story.

Both phases of the filming were a joy to me, but when the second unit shooting was completed and the mass of people that made up our main unit film crew arrived from London, I was never able to overcome the nostalgia and the remembrances of my enjoyment of the good old days of second unit.

Our first safari was to Lake Hannington, a remote lake nestled in the Rift at the foot of one sheer wall of the eastern escarpment. It is the home of a vast concentration of flamingoes, and when we topped the hill that gives the first view of this magnificent spectacle, the entire lake was pink with the soda chemical common to many lakes in the Rift, and was dotted with pin-points of red which were the scattered birds. It was midday and the flamingoes had broken up from the solid-packed concentrations that normally crowd the shores. They were feeding and were spaced upon the lake as if they had been scattered by some giant paprika shaker across the surface of a pink cake.

We had been told that the flamingo population varied considerably from month to month but surely we must have arrived at the very peak of the flocking. It was October, African spring, and banks of black rain squalls rolled above the valley, sweeping it with fast moving shadows; gaps between the clouds spotlighted the hills and trees with vivid light. Rainbows curved above the cliffs and bitter winds gusted down the escarpment and churned the lake. It was awesomely dramatic, and if we could film our little sequence of the cubs discovering the flamingoes when the sunlight was at its best, it promised to be a photographer's delight.

The ideal time for filming was just before sunset when, for some reason unknown to us, the mass of birds took wing and flew in circles above the lake. Their redness would be exaggerated by the low red sun, and the angular light and black pools of shadow on the cliffs would emphasize the drama of the scene. But each evening, black clouds scudded across the sky, and the only continuity in the light was a flat grey dullness.

Most of each day, while we waited, we spent in working with the cubs on other sequences. We were only killing time, but the experience was good for the cubs. A part of our routine required one handler to look after each lion. If something unexpected happened and three cubs went in different directions, it was necessary that there be a handler to go each way. We always took at least two sets of cubs on safari, six lions in all, and our fourth handler remained at the Naivasha lion camp, *Campi ya Simba*, as it was called in Swahili, to look after the other lions.

If a situation developed requiring additional manpower to chase down wandering lions, I left my camera and became instant animal handler.

We waited through four days for the sun to pierce the clouds at evening time. But each afternoon the banks came up thick and dark. At last, on the fifth evening the sun appeared searching through a tiny hole in the sky. We saw the shaft of light sweep slowly across the hills and approach us. For a long time it seemed as if the hole would close before the shaft arrived, or that it would pass to the south. Then the first bright edges were on the trees around us, and for eight precious minutes we were bathed in the sunset light.

I rolled my camera and shouted for the cubs, they came, performed, the sun disappeared, and in those brief eight minutes – and five long days of waiting – we completed what we had come for.

We spent one more day at Lake Hannington, then we broke camp in the afternoon with the intention of driving to our base at Naivasha. I led our small procession in my Land-Rover. Sieuwke Bisleti, who knew the way, was with me.

A few miles north the lake disappeared in a series of salt flats and marshes and the road became a faint track through grass cropped low by herds of goats.

It was late afternoon and the other vehicles were not far behind when we saw the cobra. He was a magnificent specimen nearly seven feet long, as big around as my forearm. He curved through the stubble grass with surprising speed as I circled the Land-Rover ahead to cut him off. He stopped, reared up in classic cobra pose, and spread his hood.

I knew that the other people in our caravan would want to see this spectacular snake so in spite of Sieuwke's vehement objections (she would face a lion on any terms, but wanted no part of my cobra), I manoeuvred the Land-Rover to cut off the snake each time he tried to slither away. I assured Sieuwke that we were perfectly safe. After all, he couldn't bite through a Land-Rover's metal sides, and as soon as the others had seen the snake, we would drive on and leave it in peace.

For a few times it was necessary for me to speed around quite rapidly in order to cut off the snake's retreat, and once I pulled up with a front wheel quite close. He struck in the direction of the tyre, and I clearly saw the fine jets of venom which proved Sieuwke was correct and he was, indeed, a spitting cobra. If he couldn't reach flesh in which to sink his hypodermic fangs, he could spit the venom for eight or ten feet, aimed accurately at the target's eyes. I checked the windows, they were closed. Sieuwke had seen to that.

In a few minutes, the first of our caravan drove up behind us and Hubert started to get out. I shouted through the open roof hatch that here was a cobra and to stay in the car. He grinned, and dived for his camera.

When I looked back, the cobra was just disappearing under my Land-Rover. Now I couldn't move the car. I didn't want to crush the snake (although I was later to wish to God I had). Then a shout came from the car behind. 'We see him! He's just crawled up under the Land-Rover!'

Sieuwke let out a despairing gasp. I slammed the roof hatch closed and fastened the latches.

'Now look,' I said, 'don't panic. It's perfectly safe. I had the Land-Rover dustproofed only last week in order to keep my cameras clean. I know positively that there isn't a hole underneath this car big enough for a worm to crawl through, much less a seven foot cobra.' I glanced in the back where a great pile of equipment boxes, baled tents, and film cans made a perfect lurking place for wayward snakes.

I told her confidently that the cobra would drop off the undercarriage when I had driven a few miles on the bumpy track and that there was nothing to worry about.

She was not convinced and told me the old yarn about the picnickers who had come home with an adder in their basket and had been bitten in the kitchen.

'Okay,' I said. 'Get out and ride in one of the other cars. Someone else can lead the way.'

'Get out! Are you crazy? What happens when I step down? I can't see where he is. What if I put my foot right next to him?'

I conceded the point, and we drove on.

I drove for about five miles over a treacherous track. At last we came to a flat clearing and I stopped. I had grown tired of the vague whimperings and muttered damnations from Sieuwke, and I determined to prove to her the cobra by now had deserted the ship.

I felt certain misgivings at the thought of stepping down from the car, and the dire predictions and remonstrations my plan provoked were anything but reassuring. The Marchesa painted a vivid picture of that yellowish head reaching out from underneath the car and gripping my calf. From her tone I thought perhaps she wished it would. But with a self-conscious mustering of courage I stepped down. I felt an impulse to run away, but restrained the urge and in a dashing show of nonchalance strode calmly across the sand.

I surveyed the underbody from a distance, moved closer, and eventually crawled completely around the car on hands and knees, carefully examining every niche and possible hiding place. I lifted the bonnet and searched the engine compartment and poked with a long stick into the space above the gas tank. Clearly, the cobra had left.

Sieuwke shouted to the car behind: 'Did you see it drop off?'
'No.'

'But they might easily have missed it,' I said reasonably. 'Actually, it would be more likely that they would not see it, than that they would.'

Her silence declared her disbelief.

Again, I offered her the security of another vehicle.

'I wouldn't step out of this car for all the tea in China! Now would you please close the door!'

I repeated that I had examined the underbody in detail. There was no way the snake could still be with us. But somehow, perhaps it was due to Sieuwke's nagging apprehension, I felt a secret fear. I gazed in the rear view mirrow at that pile of gear in the back and when my pants' leg flapped, touching my ankle, I nearly went up like a rocket through the closed roof hatch. The doubt was planted, and I recalled uneasily my awe at that big snake's speed and manoeuvrability on the ground.

It was noticeably quiet in the car. We came to a river crossing, and I stopped halfway into the ford. We waited for ten minutes, the bottoms of the doors awash. Surely if he still were there (although I knew he could not be) the water would flush him out.

We drove another five miles and made a stop. It was now late afternoon. In another half-hour it would be dark. 'Just to satisfy you,' I said to Sieuwke, 'I'll make another check.'

Again I crawled around, peering under the car on hands and knees. The others in the caravan pulled up and watched smiling.

I convinced myself for the second time that the snake was not an unwanted passenger. I had started to straighten up, then kneeled again, looking closely, for I had seen something that made the hair on the back of my neck go crawling like little snakes.

The main cross member of the Land-Rover's frame, just in front of the rear wheels, was a squarish tube of heavy steel. There was a hole in the tube not much larger than a silver dollar, and filling the entire space of that hole was a perfect plug of yellowish-green scales. Somehow the cobra had crawled into the cross beam and was curled up inside.

I smiled weakly and explained to Sieuwke that she was sitting about six inches above the coiled cobra, so perhaps now she should get out and change cars. I said that it was safely coiled in a part of the framework of the car with its head quite out of the way, and that it would be perfectly safe for her to step down. The Marchesa's icy glare told me very clearly she was staying put.

I began thinking of ways to get him out. My first idea was to build a fire and drive the Land-Rover over it. But only a few weeks ago we had lost a Toyota truck to a careless welder's spark and the idea didn't seem very promising. The technique might possibly have got Sieuwke unseated, which would have been a relief, but on the other hand it was more than likely she would have chosen cremation rather than to face that cobra on the ground.

Eventually I resolved to poke into the hole with the tip of a very long stick and try to drive the cobra out. I found a pole about twelve feet long and remembering vividly the speed of the cobra and feeling very vulnerable lying on my back in the sand, I checked my escape route once more. Then I gritted my teeth and poked the shiny yellowish scales with the end of the stick. They moved immediately, slithering past the hole and disappeared. Now the hole was empty. The snake, somehow, incredibly, had disappeared into the small piece of hollow frame. It seemed impossible that all of that huge snake could be jammed inside the metal tube, but there it was.

We drove on in deadly silence. I tried to make a joke, to treat the situation with lighthearted bonhomie. The lack of communication was chilling. After ten miles of bone-rattling jolts and bounces, I stopped again. Now it was dusk. I pointed my flashlight at the hole. As before, the scales were there.

Again I poked them with a pole, and again they flowed like liquid past the hole and disappeared.

Twice more I drove on and stopped. Each time the same thing happened.

We had driven for nearly forty miles since the snake had come aboard. Obviously, we couldn't carry him all the way to *Campi ya Simba*, and I couldn't park the Land-Rover on Crescent Island or anywhere else, for that matter, with the chance of leaving my deadly passenger behind. Soon we would be on the main Baringo road where it would be difficult to stage a cobra unloading operation. There was nothing for it but to get rid of him now. I stopped the car in a wide place and we parked the other vehicles so that their headlights pooled the area with light. It would be dangerous to have more than one person in the open, for they might stumble over each other in a scramble if and when the cobra did come out, so I asked everyone to stay inside. With a flashlight and a pole in my hand I began again to poke into the hole. I had now attached a long piece of springy wire to the end of the pole in the hope it would bend and flex in the same way as a plumber's snake and follow the cobra around corners, reaching into the most remote unseen crannies of the frame. It seemed to work. The wire disappeared after the retreating snake, and I thought I could feel its end shoving something soft and yielding.

While I was poking here, feeling there, on hands and knees, head down, ramming the wire into the far side of the frame where I fancied the snake had gone, I was not thinking of the other, near end of the channel. I was holding the end of the flashlight in my mouth so that I could use both hands on the pole, aiming its beam by moving my head. Suddenly in the dim peripheral glow of my light, I was aware of a movement about two feet from my ear. I turned my head up, pointing the flashlight straight into the staring face of the cobra.

I have only a very fleeting but vivid impression of the next moments. The snake made that quick jerky motion characteristic of cobras, and reared up spreading its hood. At the same time my feet were gathering under me, and I was falling backwards while simultaneously running on my heels. I crouched, feet churning, as if I were pedalling a bicycle without a frame, and making surprising speed even though I had no wheels. Then I collapsed on my back twenty feet away.

I froze as the snake continued to emerge from the open end of the frame. It seemed to come out forever, as if extruded from the metal. It was watching me with its unblinking eyes, doubtless as much afraid as I. Then it turned, made a slight grating sound against the gravel, slithered past the wheel, sped away and disappeared into the darkness.

I brought up the rear of the caravan, without my guide, for the remainder of the journey home. It was rather lonesome driving alone with no one to talk to.

★

Long before we went to the Serengeti I had discovered that all the wild lions of East Africa are not like those I had seen that first day in Nairobi National Park. Only in their universal disregard for automobiles are they the same. Lions everywhere in the parks regard cars with a degree of disinterest bordering on disdain. They seem to have the same attitude toward tourists as most of the park employees. Perhaps contempt is contagious.

Elsewhere, outside the parks, one rarely sees lions and when one does, it is usually only a fleeting glimpse as they are running away, disappearing into the bush.

Perhaps the most rewarding of all our safaris was the one to the Serengeti. There were two sections to be filmed there; one would require the main unit with Susan Hampshire and Nigel Davenport and the full contingent of technicians. When the filming of that section was completed, they would return to Naivasha, and I would spend a few days again with my beloved second unit. We had timed our arrival months ago, to coincide with the fairly predictable movements of herds of game that migrate from the north end of Mara Masai Game Reserve two hundred miles away, south through the Serengeti all the way to Ngorongoro Crater. Much of the time the herds are scattered or are lost in the bush of the west. But during early March vast herds congregate on the open grasslands of the southern Serengeti Plains. The herds are constantly moving, but from time to time they remain fairly stable in an area, circulating within the locale, fingers of animals groping away from the main, more static, palm of the herd.

In order to get some idea of the location of the animals and where we might best set up our cameras to film the sequences showing the release of the three lions, which was to take place near the herds, we flew east from Seronera looking for the main

Sieuwke Bisleti

Jack Couffer

concentration. Miles of plains were disappointingly empty. Except for the occasional Thompson's gazelle or zebra nothing moved below.

A tawny eagle flew with us for a moment, then wheeled away into a sterile void of empty blue.

Thirty elephants stood under a grove of trees that followed a glittering stream.

The herds had been reported in this area, but I was just as happy that we didn't find them here. There was too much bush and cover to photograph them effectively. One would have been unable to see the animals.

We headed south and the country began to open out. This was the edge of the Serengeti Plains, but the hills were deserted. We passed Nobby Hill and Lake Magadi and swung to the west. Now a few animals began to show as black dots against the ground. Brown hills changed to green. It was clear that this area had had rain more recently than the country we had been flying over. Dark lines and smudges began to show on the greenness up ahead, and then quite suddenly, we were over the herds.

The view from the air was of the most impressive concentration of animals I had ever seen. Indeed, it was the most impressive view of animals I will ever be likely to see, for here was the greatest collection of large animals left on earth. The total herd of wildebeest alone has been estimated at 750,000 animals, and mixed in with them were zebras and Thompson's gazelles in uncountable numbers. Of course one never sees the entire accumulation at one time, they are spread out for many miles, but the effect of that vast view was truly staggering. We circled wide, skirting low hills and flat plains, and still the herds went on – long lines of animals walking single file, strung out across the open plains, occasionally gathered in clumps like knots on black ropes casually tossed on to the grass.

It was midday by the time we had found the herds, and many stood under trees in the shade. Every thorn tree had its knot of animals beneath, a clump much larger than the shade the tree provided, so that many stood in the sun. Valleys were black with wildebeest, and along the periphery zebras made a pale grey edging, like a lighter fringe on a dark carpet thrown upon a green uneven floor.

Very soon we realized our luck. We could not have arrived at a more opportune time in the migration. If we had come here when the herds were far out in the middle of the Serengeti Plains, it would have been impossible for us to photograph them effectively. The camera had to be elevated above the herds in order to penetrate their vastness. At ground level one would only see the first few rows of animals.

But from our viewpoint the herds were spread out along a row of hills bordering the western edge of the plains, and long lines were grazing through the spectacular piles of rounded granite boulders known as *kopjes*. This was truly the most photogenic part of the Serengeti, and to have found the herds elsewhere would have been bitterly disappointing to me. Also, this was the very area where Joy and George Adamson had released Jespah, Gopa and Little Elsa. In fact we ended up filming the sequences which re-created the release less than ten miles from the site where it had actually taken place. Heretofore, when I had been asked to tell the story, I had somewhat facetiously said that it was a tale about taking three cubs to lion paradise. I realized now that this was, indeed, a paradise for animals.

We settled our unit at the nearest lodge, Seronera, nearly fifty miles from the herds, and for five days we journeyed out each morning and filmed among the animals. Somehow our crew and the transport required to move it, in spite of the most diligent efforts to hold its numbers down, had become a fleet of nearly twenty vehicles, and this grand caravan, which we came to call bitterly *The Circus*, was an ugly intrusion into this pristine landscape. I longed to be here under the same conditions as those in which we had worked when we had started our filming, with the second unit. When filming with Susan and Nigel was completed in the Serengeti, and all the crew that must of necessity accompany the kind of first-unit shooting we had been doing, had departed, I went off with my camera under my arm, with the lions and our tents, two Land-Rovers and a truck, and headed back for the herds. I was sorry that Susan and Nigel couldn't join us. They would have enjoyed it immensely. But this was the *other kind* of production, the kind that film stars never see, and the kind, unfortunately, that would have given them the most pleasure.

With special permissions we headed out from Seronera, past the *kopjes* where we had been working, beyond the end of the dirt track that was called a road, out across the open unmarked plains. I fancied that it was very like the sensation my forefathers must have experienced when heading into Kansas or the Dakotas. The only roads were the tracks of animals, such as buffalo trails over the hills; one didn't see another human being in a hundred miles. We drove deep into the country, keeping close to the hills, sometimes finding our path blocked by watercourses, and then doubling back to look for a way through, picking a granite *kopje* on the horizon to use as a landmark. Without these navigational points we would soon have been lost in these vast featureless hills. We came to the edge of the herds which had been drifting to the south now for nearly a week since I had first seen them from the air. We penetrated into the lines and bunches, searching for the heart, the nucleus of this vast, swelling and contracting, amoeba-like mass that was called a herd.

We found it late in the afternoon and set up our camp halfway down a gentle slope that divided a flat table-land from a valley that was virtually seething with game. Set back from the main path of the migration as we were, the strings of wildebeest and zebra paid no attention to us or to our tents and vehicles. The processions went on all afternoon, and far into the night we heard the peculiar snorts of the wildebeest as they filed past. Lions roared on the plateau above us, and our cubs looked out of their van curiously. We kept them inside at night.

Even though our lions were nearly a year old, and of such a size that they could now barely qualify as cubs, there was a very real likelihood that they would have been attacked if we had not protected them by putting them in their wire enclosed vans. Local lions might have gone for them out of territorial urges, and leopards or hyenas might have come for them as prey.

The next morning we went up on the table-lands above our camp and found two full-grown lionesses on a kill less than a mile from our tents. Doubtless they were the ones we had heard roaring during the night.

5 'Lights, Camera, Lions'

While Susan and Nigel and I were still in London, we had talked about lions. I didn't have any more experience with lions than they, but I did have a long background of familiarity with other wildlife, and I knew that the knowledge one learned from working with one kind of animal usually applied to other kinds as well. For this reason, I was not at all apprehensive about the seemingly difficult and dangerous undertaking of working with lions. On the other hand, there are vast differences in behaviour, of course, between different kinds of animals; between cats, for example, and dogs, just as there are profound differences of character and temperament between any different half-dozen individual dogs. On previous films I had learned, for example, that a wolf, in spite of its great resemblance to a German shepherd dog, cannot be trained with the techniques used for dogs – obedience and command – because a wolf's nature is entirely different from a dog's, and he does not have the background of familiarity with man that comes from several centuries of domesticity. A wolf must be induced – 'motivated' in the jargon of the animal handler – by other things much more subtle than retribution and reward. The same principles apply to lions and most other wild animals.

Neither Susan nor Nigel had any particular affinity for wild-life – especially not for lions. They did have a more than average curiosity and warmth for animals, but they were not deeply involved in animal lore, with households full of pets, a cat on every sofa, and a dog in front of the fireplace and another one under the dinner table. It may seem odd that we should cast artists who did not have a strong attachment for animals in parts that would require a portrayal of people who were as deeply motivated by their associations with wildlife as Joy and George Adamson, but we agreed that because Susan Hampshire and Nigel Davenport were both fine professionals, an actor and an actress in the grand tradition of 'the show's the thing!', they would be able to *act* as if they loved the lions. Indeed I felt quite sure that Susan would be able to *act* as if she didn't have any fear about kissing a full-grown lioness on the nose – one of the scenes she would eventually be required to play. We knew that it would take some time for performers and lions to become so well acquainted that there would be no apprehensions to register on film (the camera, incidentally, is very astute at picking up nuances of expression, and is hard to fool), but we didn't know how long it would be before stars and lions would come to some kind of mutual tolerance. In fact, at the end of the first day of introductions, our engaging cubs had won the love of both Susan and Nigel, and equally our stars appeared to have earned the affection of the lions.

Susan and Nigel arrived in Kenya only a week before we were to begin their filming, and we were anxious to get on with introducing them to the lions. The producer, Paul Radin, was nervous, and Carl Foreman, the executive producer, had flown in from London to be on hand in case there was trouble of some kind during these first anxious days. We all had far more apprehension about how Susan and Nigel would react to the lions than our artists had fear about meeting their co-stars. We arranged a Saturday afternoon tea party, to be held under the green-barked fever trees at *Campi ya Simba*, with its tall wire enclosures and handlers' tents where the lions were quartered. It was a beautiful location of shady clearings, grass and sunlit knolls.

We sat on camp chairs in front of the tents and the lion handlers, Hubert, Cheryl, Sieuwke, and Willy began to bring the lions down from their *bomas*, the enclosed compounds where they were kept, to meet Susan and Nigel. We certainly used a bit of obvious psychology during these preliminary introductions. First to come were the smallest cubs, Sieuwke's five from Addis Ababa. By now they had grown from the toy dog size to cubs as big as Airedales, but their personalities and antics were as naive and friendly as kittens. No one could be afraid of these warm furry things, indeed one's instant urge was to cuddle them. They had just been fed and would play for half-an-hour before settling down for their afternoon naps.

And how they played! No other animals play more wholeheartedly than lion cubs. While two were leaping and running, clutching each other, wrestling and rolling in the grass, another entered into what seemed to be his favourite routine. Stealing away and hiding in ambush, he waited for as long as he could tolerate the excrutiating suspense, crouched in the grass, belly low, ears back, tense, vibrating with the lovely anticipation of his forthcoming charge. Eventually, his mates' antics brought them closer and he stalked them, edging forward with incredible stealth (or so he seemed to think), until at last he could not suppress the pent up energy which was racing around inside him, visibly becoming more acute, swelling, a growing charge of electricity, finally bursting forth in a wild glorious attack.

When the play was over, Susan fed one of the babies from a bottle with a rubber nipple, and Nigel lay down in the grass and submitted to their investigations, their sniffings and pawings, their nippings and bitings, their obvious declarations of everlasting love.

Next, Hubert Wells, our head handler, brought out Arusha, the full-grown lioness, with whom he had his own rather special kind of love affair. He led her from her *boma* on a leash

and she came along like some great tame dog, constantly
rubbing her sides against his knees, wanting to tackle him,
using her forelimbs and paws like hands to grasp his leg
affectionately and try to hold him. Hubert tied Arusha to a
stake and we all gathered around to admire her. It would have
been pushing too hard to attempt any contact between Susan,
Nigel, and this large lioness on their first day. We did however have the opportunity to observe her complete friendliness,
and were reassured by her passivity, but in the end she
yawned, casually showing her massive teeth, and thus somewhat spoiled the illusion of harmlessness.

Weeks later, after Susan and Nigel had watched the handlers
at work with the lions during filming, and had themselves
spent hours sitting with the great cats in the intervals between
scenes, they were to assimilate a confidence and rapport with
the lions. And only a month after this first introduction, Susan
was helping the handlers by leading lions from trucks to sets,
grooming and feeding them.

After our cast had met the cubs, we talked about a few of
the basic facts, the do's and don'ts of working with lions. We
sat in the finest classroom in the world, on the grass with the
lions, in the shade, under the fever trees. We never managed
to formalize Hubert's lessons to the degree of writing them
down, and now that I am called upon to do so, the facts seem very
obvious to me and unenlightening, but for the technical
record and for those many readers who might contemplate
shooting a feature motion picture about lions, here are Hubert's
rules.

First came the don'ts. Evidently, according to Hubert's dic-
tums, one can do more things wrong with lions, than one can
do things right.

Rule 1: If one of our tame lions takes a part of you in his mouth,
an arm for example, don't pull quickly away. He will only be
'holding' you as in 'holding hands'.

The Masai Manyatta

Out walking

Rule 2: If a lion chases you, don't run. That would be the worst thing to do, because the lion will think it's only a game and will chase after you. There seems to be an instinct in a lion that makes him chase a running figure. Probably it has to do with the hunter-prey relationship.

I sensed that at this point in Hubert's talk, the atmosphere was growing slightly tense. Nigel made a remark about there seeming to be nothing one could do if attacked by a lion except stand like a post. One couldn't run. One couldn't even pull one's arm out of his maw.

Hubert agreed, and continued cheerfully.

Rule 3: Never allow any adult lion, even a large cub, to be unrestrained in the proximity of children. There is an unmistakable look in a lion's eye that goes much deeper than mere interest when watching a child. One can see it even in the attitude of a tame lion which is not at all malicious.

Again I believe it has something to do with the instinctive hunter-prey relationships. Only it has, perhaps, also something to do with *play*, which can be a danger. Certainly the many tame lions who have attacked small children have not done it out of maliciousness or hunger.

We discussed using this hunter-prey play motive in our filming, and it is not without a bit of self-condemnation of our human frailty that I now recall that we should even have thought of using it. Yet on several occasions, when the lion was required to have the most intently unblinking attitude, we did discuss using an agile child for 'bait'. We thought we would arrange the lion crew in various defensive positions, and that the child would stand beside a cage so that he could pop inside in the way a rodeo clown leaps into a barrel when charged by the bull. It was a device that gave one, even as something only considered and never used, a certain moral self-disrespect.

Rule 4: Keep face away from claws, even the paws of small cubs. (This is a specific rule for beautiful film stars, and does not apply to anyone who does not mind a few harmless but unphotogenic playful cuts and friendly scratches.)

Rule 5: Don't kneel in presence of a lion unless you want to be playfully mauled. Kneeling is an invitation to attack, and handlers frequently use the device of kneeling, or of lying on the ground, to recall a lion or to induce a charge. A lion simply can't resist the fun of running at and pouncing on, any prone or kneeling figure.

So much for the don'ts. Now, Hubert told us some of the do's.

Rule 6: In the situation previously described in *Rule 1*, when the lion has your arm in his mouth, *do* shove it in *further*. Make it uncomfortable for him to hold your arm is the principle, and he will let it go.

Nigel wondered if the same rule applied for heads as for arms. Hubert assured him that it did.

Rule 7: Be trusting, he said, but trust the handlers and not the lions. Handlers read the attitude of the lion and know each lion so well and each lion's expressions and the meanings of its expressions so perfectly that they can say if the lion is in good humour or bad. Do what we tell you to do with utter confidence. Trust us, and you will never be afraid (and the lion, at the same time, will know intuitively that you are unafraid and will not try to take some perverse advantage of your fear).

Rule 8: Lastly, spend time with the lions as frequently as possible. A half-an-hour a day, wandering through the *bomas*, spending a few minutes with each group, is sufficient. Lead the cubs around, sit around with them on location, get used to them and let them get used to you.

The tea party ended up with Susan and Nigel already perfectly at ease with the lions, and posing for the still photographers with the half-grown cubs. Even the producers, in unsolicited demonstrations of bonhomie, posed intrepidly with the lions – there under the fever trees, at *Campi ya Simba*, in Darkest Africa.

★

Many of the London technical crew eventually became lion handlers to some degree. We used no cages to keep the lions away from the technical crew and there were never guards with guns standing by. I was afraid that such precautions would give rise to an infectious psychology of apprehension. It would have been foolish, of course, not to have had the guns handy should real danger arise, but most of our filming was with the cubs, and we handled potentially hazardous scenes carefully with respect for the risks involved. Even Sieuwke, who alone and unable to help, had watched her friend, the trainer Diana Carr-Hartley, killed by a captive lion during the filming of *Hatari*, accepted the principle without question. I always wondered if a tame full-grown lion were ever to jump on me (and I would certainly not be knowingly on the loose with an un-tame one), would it be better to take one's chances with the lion, or with an excited guard trying to shoot him off my back?

Perhaps the most vulnerable thing on our location was the camera – top heavy, sitting astride three spindly legs on which it couldn't run and apparently, judging from the many times it was attacked by the lions, a tempting object of curiosity. Perhaps it was that humming-sound that made it seem alive – as Hubert would have put it: 'so that something of the hunter-prey relationship developed'. The crew was given instructions never to leave the camera unguarded. One of them must be standing by at all times to protect it from attack. It was a very vulnerable piece of equipment, and if it were knocked over on its tripod, it would surely be broken. And so, of necessity, the crew became instant lion-handlers.

I always thought the clapper-boy (low man in the camera crew hierarchy) was, perhaps, the most intrepid of the lot. He faced his first lion attack with special grace. Ace, one of the most engaging of the Middle Group, took it upon himself one day to charge the whirring camera. He came dashing toward those spindly legs and our clapper-boy bravely stood between. Ace put on the brakes and stopped in time, but he did not appreciate the clapper-boy's attitude and in frustration grabbed the first thing he could reach, and held on. It happened to be the most delicate and personal part of the clapper-boy's anatomy. I thought the lad used unbelievable restraint and astounding recall. Can you imagine under those conditions referring the *Rule 1*? He stood rooted, surprised, white-faced, and still, and with remarkably casual British aplomb, remarked 'Oh! Quite!'

This trait of the lions to lie in ambush and then spring out and charge was surely a playful ramification of what in the wild would be refined by parental training to become the hunting charge. In our lions the urge was doubtless as much a part of them as whiskers and claws; something in their genes told them this was a part of lion behaviour and until the activity was redirected into hunting, it remained only a playful, albeit sometimes irritating, and frightening part of lion character. When we walked our lions in the forest, we were constantly aware of the imminent surprise charge from ambush, the little teeth and the clinging claws. If it came from behind, it came silently, and one usually ended up flat on one's face in the grass.

But it is by developing and embellishing traits such as this, that we have been able to coax lions as well as other animals to perform in films. The words, *training, conditioned response, behavioural reinforcement, operant conditioning,* are only attempts to describe a way to adapt or refine a characteristic which is already part of an animal's instinctive behaviour. Sometimes an individual animal is seen to have a special idiosyncrasy which one can amplify or modify in order to fit a specific film situation. This kind of circumstance would be the closest thing we do to what is called training.

But the people who help us with animals in films are not really so much *trainers* (although that is what we sometimes call them), as they are students of animal behaviour, and as behaviourists *motivation* is a most important part of their vocabularies. *How do we motivate this or that lion to do thus and so?* Many animals are most easily motivated by food. They can be moved from here to there with food, and eventually, through association, just the sight of a food pan or the sound of two feeding dishes knocked together will bring forth a reaction. This most simple, basic motivation can be used in many ways.

One can get the lion to go from a place where there is no food to a place where there is food. But unless the scene we want to film requires the animal to end up eating, it can be a worthless technique, and at best is a motivation which only fits certain situations. Obviously if a lion is motivated by food and is lured to food he is going to eat it when he gets there, and this is usually an undesirable action from the photographer's point of view. In spite of this there are many ways in which one can use the food motivation successfully.

Two of the most common remarks I hear in regard to my work are: 'You must have a lot of patience', and 'How do you get animals to do all of those things?'

In regard to the first remark, I'll only repeat the comment in reply to a similar query from a commercial fisherman I once filmed off the coast of California. 'It ain't the patience, it's the time. If you ain't got the patience, it takes the time anyway.'

How we succeed in getting them to do all of those things is best illustrated by an example. Let's take a hypothetical script description:

104. EXT.   GRASSY HILL AND TRAP.   DAY.

JESPAH enters from frame right, goes to trap hidden beside tree. He sniffs around, puzzled by the suspicious situation, looks warily into branches overhead. He hears GOPA calling from the right, glances toward him, starts off in GOPA's direction. Now he hears LITTLE ELSA calling behind him. He looks back and forth trying to decide which way to go and finally, having made up his mind, exits toward her.

Let us examine how we could shoot this entire scene by using only the basic food motivation. All the actions must be performed, of course, exactly on cue, at the proper time, with the expressions as described in the script.

Before shooting the scene the handlers would need a few minutes on the set with the lions for rehearsal. From a position outside the point where Ace, who we will assume is playing the part of Jespah for this scene, is to enter the picture, he would be called several times to the spot under the tree where he is to react suspiciously to the trap. Each time he comes here, he finds a cube of fresh meat on the ground. In the rehearsals he finds the meat in the same place every time. Once the lions have learned their basic training, this kind of simple reinforcement usually takes only four or five rehearsals on the set. Now Ace is ready for filming. As the handlers describe it, he has learned a routine, or he has formed a pattern of behaviour.

Now when the magic word 'Action!' is spoken, Ace enters and goes to the place beside the tree where he expects to find the meat. But this time none is there. Instead he notices a strange, rather curious odour (after-shave lotion or cologne). He looks around, puzzled. Then the hears a sound in the tree above, the very slight rattle of a feeding dish, and he looks up. He sees nothing, and does not hear the noise repeated. The sound that attracted his glance was made by a feeding dish tied in the tree and jiggled ever so slightly by a tug on a piece of invisible nylon fishing line.

Now having completed the first two movements of the scene, the script went on to say that Jespah hears Gopa calling to him from off-stage (that is from out of sight of the camera). At this point a handler, hidden behind a bush in Gopa's direction, rattles a feed dish. Ace looks toward the sound, the handler stands up beckoning with the dish enticingly, and Ace starts off toward him. But at this moment, Ace hears another feeding dish being rattled even more temptingly loud from behind, and he stops, staring back over his shoulder. He looks back and forth between the two handlers, wondering who is offering the best deal, as it were. Handler number one now shifts the feeding pan, holding it so that Ace can see that it is empty. Ace looks back at handler number two who at this moment reveals a tempting chunk of meat in his pan. Ace dashes off for the meat, exiting with the proper expression of decision in the right direction.

In this imaginary example we have played the entire scene by using only the food motivation. In actual practice, we would have complicated the motives considerably in order to get more subtle nuances of performance from our lion star.

Routines like this actually seem to be quite enjoyable for the lions, as nearly as one can interpret their emotions. They get their food as they work, and this makes it fun for them to work. Certainly they enjoy the variety of life that comes from filming, in contrast to the boredom of a daily routine, and there is no doubt that they genuinely look forward to the rides in the lion vans, the new locations, and the interesting situations. There is an aspect of animal behaviour seen in zoos where animals pace along their walls, picking each other bald, and show other evidences of boredom, which never occurred at *Campi ya Simba*. I have heard, incidentally, that at some zoos regular situations are presented to the animals in irregular ways in order to help relieve the monotony; the animals are fed, for example, at a different time each day so that the small pleasure of anticipation, one of the few satisfactions left to caged animals, does not become a monotonous routine.

*

Hubert discovered very early that he could not simply assign certain of his handler-assistants to be in charge of specific lions. Instead of handlers choosing the lions with which they would like to work, the lions, in fact, chose their handlers.

Each of the lions had his favourite person, and this was another aspect of motivation which we used to help the lion-stars introduce subtleties into their performances. In the scene which I have described, and which we theoretically solved by using the food motivation exclusively, it would have made considerable difference which handler was at what point. In fact, if we had actually filmed such a scene food might have been left out of the motivation entirely and we might have used a lion's affection for one handler – his response to a familiar voice or odour – played off against his lack of interest in another handler for our effect. Food is not always a useful motivation. The lions aren't always hungry, and a lion that is playing for food has a *food* look in his eye. All of the basic feelings are called upon to get performances from lions, just as they are used by human actors. And different animals, of course, respond differently to different motivations. Lions in general react very strongly to three basic senses: sight, hearing, and smell, and that is one of the reasons they are excellent film performers. Another reason is their strong social sense. A lion in the wild is a part of a pride, a closely welded family group. We discovered that with our lions a *person* can become a part of a pride. In much the

Arusha

same way that Konrad Lorenz has described the relationship of certain wolf-like dogs which respond to their owners as pack-leaders, our handlers became the pride-leaders of our lions.

The different backgrounds and attitudes of our handlers in regard to this situation were, I think, responsible in great degree for our success with the lions. No one single approach would have worked quite so well as the combination of ideas that resulted from their differences.

Hubert Wells is a professional handler of animals for films and he began this work over fifteen years ago before he left his native Hungary. He is analytical, and he makes a serious study of animal behaviour. One had the feeling that he sat up nights on end thinking of new ways to get our lions to do new and astounding things.

On another picture, one of the most challenging problems I had ever faced with animals in films was solved by Hubert, but only after what must have been many sleepless nights. When making the film *Ring of Bright Water* we worked with what I am sure are the most difficult animals of all to film. An otter's face, although bright, seems fixed in its somewhat devilish expression. This was a problem because it was difficult to get different meaningful expressions. But to further our exasperation, we soon discovered that an otter is motivated by nothing as strong as its native curiosity, and when introduced to a strange location no sound, no food, no smell, no movement, seemed to overpower his vast capacity for exploration.

We found that an otter is forever on the move, always trotting with that peculiar humping gait, exploring here, investigating something on this side of the set, then running off to examine something at the other side, and we found it nearly impossible to make him stay still long enough to take a picture of his charming, albeit fixed-expression, face.

There is one characteristic pose that an otter strikes when he is curious about something he cannot see. Because he is so short-coupled, he must often rise up and stand on hind legs in order to look over a hillock or see above the grass. This moment when an otter is erect on hind legs is the only opportunity when a cinematographer can depend on catching him standing still. It is, also, a very charming pose. Hubert's problem was how to convince Oliver, the leading otter of the film, and the one that showed the most inclination toward this attitude, that I was the director, and when I said I wanted him to stand up in a given spot at a certain time, he ought, at least, to give full consideration to the notion of complying.

Hubert eventually discovered a rare treat to which Oliver reacted with at least mild interest: fresh crab meat. Thus developed a refinement of the basic food motivation which enabled us to accomplish the remarkable feat of getting an otter to stay and stand on command. It took three months to perfect the routine.

First Hubert fed the otter each day on a pedestal a foot high and eight inches in diameter. This platform was used as a point of reference for the otter, something which could be put in place at a given spot – much as an actor's chalk mark is drawn on the floor of a set. In order to get his dinner Oliver was asked to climb onto the pedestal and stand up, reaching for the food in Hubert's hand above his head. While Oliver was eating, Hubert gave a command: 'Oliver, up!' The otter finally learned to go to the pedestal and stand up for his food, and eventually he found it easier to remain balanced in the upright position accepting the morsels as Hubert offered them. In this way, Oliver learned to stay upright for longer intervals than the short moments he would ordinarily remain in this position, and eventually he would stand on his pedestal for nearly a minute waiting to be fed.

Hubert had completed step one of Oliver's training. But we couldn't take his picture on the pedestal. The film wasn't about a circus and the pedestal was hardly a suitable set decoration for shots of an otter in the wilds of the Scottish Highlands where the movie was to be filmed. Hubert therefore began to scale down the pedestal, gradually sawing it off bit by bit, until eventually that foot-high platform of wood became a flat round piece of sacking on which Oliver perched to be fed, a bit of cloth which could be hidden on a set and to which Oliver would run and stand when Hubert shouted the familiar command.

This was Hubert's method: methodical, calculated, accomplished. He had absolute respect and regard for the animals: kindness was a part of his professionalism. Not only would unkindness be immoral, it would work against the results of his job. It would not be good for the animals, and therefore it would not be good for him.

Sieuwke Bisleti, on the other hand, was completely intuitive in her approach. At first she was suspicious of Hubert's analytical techniques. She had heard about *trainers* and thought of them as caricatures of men with pistols on their belts, tall shiny boots, and long black whips. She soon put that concept aside. Sieuwke is not a professional animal handler – that is she does not earn her living from year to year by working with animals. She grew up in Indonesia and raised her baby daughter in a Japanese prisoner of war camp. Later, she lived all over the world, learning languages as she travelled; then she met the Italian Marchese whom she married. During all the fifteen years she has lived in Kenya, animals have been a part of her household: bucks, lion cubs, leopards, jackals, any orphaned or injured youngsters that were brought to her from the bush. She is mother to them all, and they come when she calls. They play together and find a home until they are ready to return to the wild from which they came. She does all this because she enjoys helping animals and having them around her house. She is *Mum*, and her whole approach to the husbandry and training of animals is that of a woman, a mother.

Cheryl Shawver's approach is just about dead centre
between Hubert's and Sieuwke's. She is an American girl, only
twenty-five-years old, and is already unswervingly professional,
knowledgeable and competent. She has Hubert's reasons for
working with animals – as an occupation, a way to make a
living doing what she enjoys. As a professional she is able to
detach herself from the emotional aspects of dealing with
animals, but at the same time she has Sieuwke's womanly
intuition.

Our fourth handler, Willy Roberts, is a Kenya lad who
grew up at Lake Baringo, a remote area on the edge of the
desert north, the wild Northern Frontier District. Her father, until
he died two years before Willy came to us, had been known over
the whole of Kenya as the most authoritative expert at capturing
and exporting wild birds, and Willy's mother has continued the
business and is one of the few people still allowed by the
conscientious Kenya government to collect wild birds. Willy's
experience in the bush was as important to us as his expertise
in dealing with animals.

Perhaps a good illustration of different approaches to animals
is shown in the way Hubert and Sieuwke called their lions.
When Hubert wanted to call Arusha, the full-grown lioness
that was his special pride, he rang a bell. When Sieuwke
wanted to bring her five, she imitated the notes of a mother
lioness recalling her cubs. She had learned this call from her
own lioness, Sheeba, and her imitation was uncannily true.
It was strange to watch Sieuwke from afar, walking through
the African bush, tailed by five cubs, and hear her various soft
calls as she spoke to them in their own language. The '*baow!*'
and the '*unh-hungh!*' that obviously has some special meaning
for a lion cub.

It would have been perhaps equally odd for a stranger
unaccustomed to the bizarre ways of animals handlers, to have
come unexpectedly upon Hubert walking through the bush,

Susan Hampshire with Ace

Hubert Wells and Cheryl Shawver
with Arusha

Hubert Wells and the pride

Sieuwke Bisleti and her cubs

Susan Hampshire brought her baby,
Christopher, to Africa

Susan Hampshire and a Masai

carrying a dry-cell battery and a coil of wire, pushing a brass button, and ringing an electric doorbell.

Often visitors to our sets were amazed to see our two lady lion handlers leading half-grown cubs, alternately dragging and being dragged by the lions eager to begin the play of performing before the camera – or to see the women chasing after a lion who had decided to visit his mates half a mile away, or the cub who had thought it might be interesting to run down the hill and have a look at a cattle herd. There they would go, trying to head him off, girls running like mad through the bush, leaping over cactuses like boys, their hair flying wildly in the wind.

6 Masai

When I arrived to film *Living Free*, my first impressions of Africa were far different from those romanticized notions I had previously held. In most of the motion pictures I had seen with East African backgrounds one was shown only the picturesque side of the little thatched huts, not the back view with the rusty tin patches and the bad sanitation. Ours was a story of modern East Africa, and so I determined that I must show it as it really is. Later as I grew familiar with more remote places, I discovered that there really are two completely different kinds of Africa, and that when one gets off the beaten track, things are very much as they were a hundred – or a thousand – years ago.

We would be working at considerable length with people of the Masai tribe, one of the semi-nomadic herding tribes, who occupy vast tracts of land in both Kenya and Tanzania. I first met a Masai when I was in East Africa for only a few days, taking a quick course in local geography. With Philip Leakey, a son of the famous archaeologists, I drove over three thousand miles in about two weeks, most of them at alarmingly high speeds over distressingly rough and dusty tracks. I didn't get to know the country very well in the course of that whirlwind tour but a good part of me got on very intimate terms with the hard seat of a Land-Rover. The trip however laid some of the ground-work and enabled me to discover, however superficially, the areas to which I would return to make more detailed surveys.

One night we were coming back from a trip that had taken us through Tsavo National Park, along the northern foothills of Kilimanjaro, and through Amboseli Game Reserve. A good deal of this survey had been *bundu crashing*, that is leaving the tracks altogether and driving right through the bush. We had bashed the car across several very thorny areas and had used up all our spare tyre patches while repairing what seemed to be a gross of punctures. Shortly after dark another thorn worked through the tyre and soon we felt the now familiar sag and wobble of a flat. By this time we were back on what passed for a road, but there was very little likelihood of seeing another car. A couple of hours earlier, we had come round a sharp bend and had quite unexpectedly run into a flock of guinea fowl. One of the birds had bounced off the front fender, and we had picked up the carcass. Resigned to spending the night in the bush, we chopped some wood with a *panga*, the ubiquitous heavy knife of Africa, and prepared to have barbecued fowl for dinner. We had no camping gear with us, but the night was warm, the fire was bright, the grass was soft, and the stars were all we would need to cover us. I was almost grateful for the excuse to relax and forget the business of film making.

We had no more than just kindled the fire in a clearing a hundred feet from the road, than we heard the sound of a car approaching. It would be an unexpected bit of good fortune if we could get help to repair our tyre. Phil ran out in the road and stood waving his arms as a pair of shuddering yellow headlights swept around a curve. It was a little open truck, the cab crowded with staring faces, driven by a turbaned trader. Phil spoke for a moment to the driver, then I saw him heave in the wheel with the flat and climb up after it. He shouted from the rear as the truck lurched ahead: 'I'll get this fixed in Sultan Hamud and be back when I can.' Then he disappeared into the dust and darkness. What he had said didn't mean much to me. I didn't even know where Sultan Hamud was, and in any event he certainly couldn't return before morning. I turned back to the fire and my guinea fowl. The bird was plucked and impaled on a green stick which I turned occasionally. It sizzled and drops of fat splashed and sputtered onto the red coals.

I sat with my chin in my hands, staring into the hypnotic

flames. A hyena called from somewhere off in the darkness, with its strange, quickly ascending notes that are not at all a laugh. Then vaguely, I became aware that I was not alone. There was a movement in the grass across the fire, and I realized that an animal was there in the darkness just outside the fireglow, watching me. I froze, trying to decide quickly whether it was a lion or a leopard. Then I saw it move again, and realized it was a dog. I called, made some friendly gestures, and it came, followed immediately by another. Then from the blackness strode a tall figure. He planted the butt-end of a polished steel spear over five feet long into the ground beside the fire, spoke to me a few words that sounded like nothing I had ever heard before, and sat on his haunches opposite the fire. I said hello to him in English, which of course he could not understand. I recognized at once that he was a young Masai, a warrior, perhaps the most singular-looking man I had ever seen.

His hair was braided into many small plaits, the whole of it plastered with a reddish clay. His ear lobes were punctured and greatly elongated, spangled with triangular pieces of metal, and in the loop of one ear he carried a small round box. He wore a belt that held a sword-like knife, and a piece of dull-red cloth was thrown over his left shoulder. It did very little towards covering his body. His right breast and most of his left side were bare. In effect, he was naked. His entire body was of the same ruddy colour as his hair. It had been lightly smeared with a mixture of red clay and grease, and his breast was adorned with a delicate pattern of welts and scars. He wore bracelets of wire, beads, and leather, and a tight choker-collar of bright red and blue beads and pearly white shell buttons. Spare, long muscled, smiling, features finely chiselled, he was incredibly handsome. Crouching there in the fireglow opposite him seemed at the moment, in spite of the incongruity, the most natural thing in the world.

He · began to talk to me in what I assumed must be the

Masai language; but to me it all sounded like one great long word strung together without pauses in between. I said a few things in English, just to let him know that we were fighting a serious problem of communication, and began to try out my sign language. I felt that anyone who walked through the night with dogs must have an affection for his animals and this seemed to be the best place to start. I patted the dogs, nodding approval. I thought his signs confirmed that he understood my appreciation, but perhaps I was reading things into his nods and gestures which had not been meant.

The *panga*, a broad-bladed knife used everywhere in Africa for anything from hacking brush to cutting throats, which I had used for cutting the firewood was lying at his feet. He picked it up and studied it carefully, examining the handle in meticulous detail and testing the sharpness of the blade. He tried it out, neatly splitting a piece of log, nodded approvingly, then held it possessively looking at me across the fire. Obviously he thought it was a good *panga*.

I must here admit that a certain uneasiness began to creep into the situation. I realized my disadvantage. Here I was lost in the middle of the night, God knew where, in possession of goods which might be thought by a Masai, who was poor in those things which we consider to be great material value, to be a carload of vast wealth. I stared across the fire at what I fancied was an unsophisticated wildman who held all the weapons. I began to read things into those curious stares and calculating glances. Was he deciding whether to split me up the middle, or carve me crosswise? Would he use the spear first, or the *panga*? As I was thinking this, he reached for the spear, and I marvelled at the way it became a part of him. The long fluted blade glistened along the edges where it had been recently honed. He handled it as if it were an extension of his body, not yet to impale me, but only to reach out and flick a bit of wood from four feet away with its tip into the fire. He planted it again, standing it shuddering and glinting in the firelight.

We sat opposite each other for fifteen minutes, unspeaking, thinking our private thoughts. I decided at last to put the situation to test. If he were going to kill me, let him do it now. I figured if he could examine my *panga*, then surely I could look at his spear! I got up and pulled it out of the sand. He didn't seem to mind. In fact he wasn't at all worried, but was watching me with the widest grin I had seen all evening. Maybe he was even proud that I was interested in his spear. Anyway, it was obvious that I had done the right thing. I hefted it and tested its edge (which, as I suspected, was as sharp as a razor).

He chucked down the *panga* and took the spear from me, held it by its wooden mid-piece in throwing position and flexed his arm quickly so that both long metal ends vibrated excitingly. I realized he was demonstrating the way to judge the quality of a spear. Obviously this was a good one which vibrated properly, and he was proud of it. I took it back and imitated his motion. The spear vibrated for me, too, but not so grandly. Nevertheless, I was delighted that I had succeeded, and it seemed to delight him.

Now that all thought of threat was out of mind, I replaced the spear and returned to sit by the fire. The guinea hen needed turning, and I thought perhaps the reason my new friend had joined me was to share my meal – something of the age-old custom of dividing food over the fire. I patted one of the dogs again, confirming my friendliness. He picked up the *panga* and pointed back and forth between dog and knife. I realized that he was proposing a trade. I made signs declining, but either he didn't understand or didn't want to. He was quite insistent with this offer to barter, but I really had no desire to own his dog. Finally, I went around to the other side of the fire again and proposed with signs that if he really wanted to trade, I would exchange the *panga* for his spear. This suggestion was not on at all. When he finally understood my proposal, he flooded me with a barrage of language. Then remembering that I could not understand, he pantomimed, thrusting at an imaginary target with the spear, at the same time repeating the word *Simba* several times. He made it very clear that he needed the spear to kill lions. I knew he didn't want to swap, but it sounded like a weak excuse to me.

We sat in silence around the fire, black man, white man, and dogs, watching the wild bird roasting over the coals. There was something understood between us, some primitive kinship lost in time, I fancied; definitely a rapport. The firelight flickered across his face and in the eyes of his dogs, and it could have been a thousand years ago. I was out of place here, but somehow at the moment I felt very much a part of it all.

The guinea fowl grew dark brown on its spit, and the fat dripped in small explosions onto the hot rocks. At last I drew it off and tore it into halves. I offered a side to the Masai, but he refused. I was surprised, because I had thought that was what he had been waiting for, and then I remembered that Phil had told me the Masai do not eat wild meat – only cattle and goat flesh, and that on special occasions. Their diet is blood drawn from the neck of living cattle, mixed with milk, and curdled with cow urine and ashes. Their entire life is organized around their herds – food, wealth, even their houses are constructed with a solid plaster of cattle dung. Phil had explained that the preoccupation of the Masai with cattle is a part of what has accounted for the continued existence of wildlife in their reserves. The Masai tradition of living side-by-side with the herds of plains game, along with their fiercely protective attitudes about intrusion onto their lands by other tribes, has allowed the wildlife to flourish in these vast tracts, whereas the wild animals elsewhere have been killed off by

agriculturists and their encroachment. Because of the wealth of
wildlife on Masai lands, the tracts have fairly recently been
declared reserves. But Masai, along with all other people, have
flourished too, and because cattle are their wealth, their flocks
have also increased. There is great irony in the situation. Vast
areas which are over-grazed by both wildlife and domestic
herds, are now becoming barren dust flats. The lands on which
wild animals were protected by Masai tradition, have now
become overpopulated and are not good for either animals or
the Masai.

When I remembered Phil's discussion, I realized the reason
the Masai had refused to share my wild meat barbecue. I
found a box of emergency rations in the car and, while I
munched ancient wild game before the fire, the Masai ate a
can of cold baked beans and drank a hot Coke.

He sat for another hour by the dying coals, then, quite
suddenly, without preamble, he got to his feet, spoke a few
words which I imagined must have been goodbye, picked up
his spear, and disappeared with his dogs back into the darkness
he had come from.

A few days later, I was to meet another Masai who
confirmed my high regard for these self-possessed and handsome people. Again with Phil Leakey, we were exploring the
wild country to the south of Suswa, when we came onto an
attractive Masai girl walking along the track carrying empty
calabashes. The waterhole for which she was heading was
several miles away, and she asked us for a lift. She sat in the
back of the Land-Rover chatting with Phil in a mixed vocab-
ulary of Swahili and her tribal tongue, unselfconscious,
friendly, but at the same time reserved, in absolute command
of herself and the situation. There was an enviable self-
possessed quality about this girl. She was aloof, but at the
same time warm – completely natural and friendly. The thing
which struck me most, was her use of touch, which we

A Masai in the bush

Sunset at
Lake Naivasha

Elephants
in Manyara

Impala

Marabou
storks

European people so rarely use. I have never had a new acquaintance in a European community touch me when engaging me in a first conversation, and if I had, I would probably have resented it. But this girl's hands were on my bare arm and shoulder repeatedly as she bantered, a cool dry hand that carried with it an aura of instant rapport. It is a very subtle thing, this quality of touching, which we Europeans do not understand, and in Nairobi one frequently sees two grown men in business suits walking down the street holding hands. In other parts of the world they would be ridiculed. Here, it only means that they are friends.

Later on, we asked a group of Masai to build a *manyatta*, a Masai village of huts with its surrounding fence of thorns, in a particularly pictorial location where we wished to film. They lived at the edge of the reserve near Naivasha and were more Europeanized than those first Masai I had met. The tall young leader of the group, who looked so completely unsophisticated with his piece of cloth over one shoulder, his nudity, beaded ear lobes, and his spear, I discovered later owned a lorry on which he had a leasing contract in Nairobi. It was amusing to see him in his near-nakedness, standing tall above his brothers, and interpreting my directions by translating them from English, through Swahili, to Masai, and speaking into an electrified power megaphone.

This *manyatta* was completed with exaggerated respect for authenticity, and the people were actually living in it with their livestock when we began filming. On the first day of photography, I noticed a peculiar scene being enacted on the sidelines. A team of magazine reporters and photographers were visiting the set and one of them had persuaded our prop man to pose for pictures. We had previously made a dozen imitation Masai spears with rubber tips to be used in a specific scene where the Masai were to be filmed chasing and throwing at the cubs. The still picture being posed was of our prop man handing out an armload of these phony spears to the villagers, and it irked me that after all our careful regard for authenticity such a photograph was being made. Out of context or without explanation, it would surely give the impression that we were being less than genuine. If it appeared in a national magazine it would make us look like caricatures of a film unit – a bunch of phonies. I stormed over and demanded that the picture should not be made, giving at the same time a full explanation of my reasons, and pointing out that it wasn't very gracious to cut one's host's neck in this insulting way.

An hour later, I saw a similar scene being re-enacted, only this time instead of rubber props, the photographer had collected an armload of real spears in the village and was photographing the prop man, as if we had brought all the spears from England, handing out their own genuine spears to authentic Masai warriors. The photographer declared a misunderstanding, but the picture would have been equally misleading, in its way. Happily I found one sharp Masai spear left uncollected and soon made it indelibly clear whom I would stick it into and where, if I ever saw the photographer again on our set.

★

Early on in our filming at the Masai *manyatta* it became evident that if things continued as they were going, we would soon be destitute of genuine Masai props and costumes. Our crew members took great fancy to the handsome beadwork, the neck chokers, arm bands, anklets and other ornaments and the best spears, *simis*, and bows and arrows were purchased and bartered for and nearly on their way to London even before the first shots were made. In order to protect the authentic beauty we had come to film, I was forced to make a ruling that there would be no trading until we had finished filming in Masailand. After that it would be open shopping, and every man for himself.

I didn't hear about one peculiar result of my ultimatum until later, and fortunately neither did Susan Hampshire. One of the crew members took a particular fancy to the spear of a Masai named Taiswa. Taiswa, in turn, had his appreciative eye on our star. The price to a Masai for a good woman is measured in numbers of cattle – to be offered a wife in exchange for a spear was a bargain beyond imagination. The oldest con-game on earth came to the mind of one of our crew. It was like walking up to a stranger on the street and offering the Brooklyn Bridge for sale. I am ashamed to reveal that our crew member thought he could perpetrate such a felony on the innocent Masai. The trade was arranged – Susan Hampshire in exchange for one polished Masai spear, and the deal was to be concluded with the actual exchange of merchandise at the end of the last day's shooting – and with no handling of the goods beforehand. There must have been other persons later involved in this illicit collusion. (Susan reported with surprise that she was rushed roughly and unceremoniously from the set that last day by her ordinarily courteous and overly solicitous driver.)

We might have departed Masailand in the classic style of old African movies, in a cloud of flying spears and a shower of falling arrows, had it not been for the fact that Taiswa was a much more sophisticated Masai than our crew member was a clever trader. Taiswa loudly and emphatically claimed deceit when he saw the Land-Rover carrying his bride-to-be disappear into the dust. He demanded the goods in a loud voice, emphasizing his claim with a mightily convincing show of his passion.

His spear was raised and quivering, and he snatched up his buffalo-hide shield and beat on it in a frenzied way that struck a bit of terror in us all. The poor crewman who had thought it humorous to play practical jokes on the naive Masai locked himself in a Land-Rover and cowered on the floor. A dozen Masai warriors leaped forward and restrained their passionate brother, but they could not hold back the frenzy of a man gone wild.

Then Taiswa laughed, and we realized it was our crewman who had been played the joker. The Masai, of course, had known all along, and had beaten him at his own game.

★

When we were on safari in Amboseli, we met other Masai who were like that first to whom I had talked in sign language across the fire.

I had heard something about the part lions played in Masai culture and mythology, and I knew that in the old days a boy did not become a man until he had participated in a hunt during which a lion was killed by a spear. It was because of the Masai's great interest in lions that we hired Masai men at *Campi ya Simba* to help with the husbandry and training, and as *askaris* to guard the *bomas* during the night. But in modern times when lions are not so numerous as they used to be in Amboseli and are closely protected, the Masai must find it very difficult to kill a lion with a spear and achieve a proper manhood, although undoubtedly they still do so when they can.

Word soon travelled through the reserve about the strange company of people who were camped below the village of Loitokitok with half-a-dozen tame lions.

Early one morning an ancient man arrived in company with a boy of about twelve years of age. They stood at a respectful distance, watching us preparing our breakfast. One of our camp helpers eventually noticed the pair and began talking with them. He discovered that the old Masai had heard about our camp through the 'bush telegraph' – that disorganized but effective news medium of Africa, by which word is passed from one traveller to another, from one village to another, never official but always fairly dependable and surprisingly rapid.

The old man said he had brought the boy to see the lions; they had left their village early the previous morning, and had walked all day, over thirty miles, and slept in the bush. We appreciated their interest, and extended ourselves to make the pair welcome and show them all they had travelled so far to see. The old man said he had brought the boy only to show him the cubs, but I think the news on the bush telegraph that night carried added embellishments: about women who actually wrestled with lions, led them around on leashes, lay down with them in the grass, and had no fear. All this must have been mightily strange to a Masai man, who reckons that his superiority to women is in part due to his ability to master lions. What a blow to his vanity to watch two women who treated lions as if they were puppies, and had even been seen to spank a young *simba* and give it a stern and sober chastising for unsheathing a claw at the wrong time.

7   Judy

It had been more than eight months since Marchesa Sieuwke Bisleti had received those first five cubs from Ethiopia and had begun rearing them. They had started out in the film playing the small trio, had gone through the transitional size, and then had grown into a position in the cast as the middle-sized group. They were as varied a lot as any five children one would find in a school classroom. Francis, the bold one, played the part of Jespah in the film. Dawn and Dennis played his sister and brother. It was remarkable how the personalities of those three lions fitted Joy Adamson's descriptions of the three cubs, Jespah, Gopa and Little Elsa, the characters in her book which our cubs were now portraying.

The two other Ethiopian cubs, Homerus and Judy, the ones our producer had seen born at Addis Ababa, were back-ups and doubles for the others. Judy was perhaps the most beautiful of them all, with perfect conformation and a grace of movement that was unique among the other, clumsier cubs. All of them had the dark marks characteristic of the Ethiopian strain.

If Dennis was the noisiest cub, the most independent, the one who was invariably first into trouble, first to get into the soup as it were, then Judy was the shyest. Judy was not a delicate lion, quite the contrary; she was physically very husky, only her personality was timid and fragile.

Because Sieuwke had raised her and had been with her from the beginning, Judy attached herself completely to her. Later Cheryl and Susan were able to meet Judy on some degree of common ground, and she came to them for stroking. But neither myself nor the two male trainers were in her favour or affection, and when it came time to call her back after a scene before the cameras, only Sieuwke or Cheryl would qualify.

Her timidity was a trait that was not at all helpful for most of our filming requirements, and because of this she did not appear in as many scenes as her contemporaries. But there were times when that shy attitude was required for a film sequence, and on those occasions where apprehension was the mood, her special quality shone like a star.

The Ethiopian cubs were eight months old when filming was completed, still playing the parts of middle-sized cubs. We had decided to give them to Lion Country Safari, and send them to America along with the other lions who would soon be returning to their home there. There is always a feeling of let-down when after months of work and the nearly total absorption that filming requires, the shooting of a film is completed. Tensions taper off, friends in the cast and crew say goodbye and drift away, and one must leave the places one has grown fond of, the animals and people for whom one has found affection.

It was with great sadness that we led the cubs into the special aluminium flight crates which were to take them to their destination. Because of limited space allowances on airplanes, we divided the cubs into seven shipments, sending three or four cubs twice a week. Gradually the number of cubs at *Campi ya Simba* diminished until, finally, only Judy and Francis remained.

We closed the doors on those last two crates, put them aboard the covered lorry that would carry them to Nairobi International Airport, and looked at each other sadly, realizing that now for sure it was over. Only Paul Radin, Eva Monley (the production manager), myself and the handlers remained. In a few days all of us would be catching different planes heading in different directions.

We went to the barren office in the old farm building that had now been stripped of everything but a disconnected telephone. It sat forlornly on the empty floor. I couldn't remember that instrument being silent for one minute in the past eight months. This wasn't the cheerful, busy room it had been throughout the production – not the place for us now. We wandered back to the empty lion camp, sat in front of Hubert's tent, and had a drink.

Three hours later I was packing my camera for the last time when I heard the familiar sound of the lion lorry. It was back from Nairobi much too soon. Something must be wrong. The sad saga of Judy began with the driver's first sentence. He told us that he had stopped halfway to Nairobi to check his load. The first thing he saw was the door of an empty lion crate swinging open. Somewhere in the thirty miles between *Campi ya Simba* and his stopping place, the door had worked its way loose and Judy had leaped from the truck. We took four vehicles and set out immediately to search the roadsides.

The highway from Naivasha to Nairobi is the main paved artery leading north-west, eventually reaching Lake Victoria and Uganda. It is a much used highway, one of the best there is by African standards, and traffic is fast.

We had not gone two miles when we realized the hopelessness of our undertaking. Most of the area between Lion Camp and the place where the driver had stopped was uninhabited bush and plain. Near Mount Longonot there were a few scattered huts and cultivated plots, but by far the greater part of the area was wild African bush. If the lost lion had been any other one but Judy there would have been a chance the cub would have approached the first human being it encountered. This could have been good or bad depending on the circumstances. An inexperienced person, particularly a child, in confronting a tame lion cub could get hurt. On the other hand, in the right circumstances, this hypothetical situation would result in our cub finding a person who would help it return to *Campi ya Simba*.

But neither situation would occur with Judy. Her natural

Masai, fascinated by the lions, came from
miles away to see them

Scenes from the film:

Susan Hampshire and a Masai trying to protect
the goats from hungry lions

Python attacking lion cub

Susan Hampshire and Nigel Davenport
with their co-stars

Susan Hampshire and Jespah

Fierce baboon traps Susan Hampshire
in her Land-Rover

Jespah, Gopa and Little Elsa facing a new
life in the Serengeti

timidity would drive her away from strangers, and now that she was in the frightening circumstance of being on her own, she would be even more afraid. There was no worry that she would hurt a human being; if she saw a stranger she would simply vanish into the bush.

We spaced our cars a few miles apart along the road in order to cover as much of the territory as we could and drove back and forth along the highway. We looked into culverts and searched patches of bush. Sieuwke and Cheryl stopped and called at regular intervals along the road, hoping their familiar voices would tempt Judy from hiding. But their shouts were pitifully small in the wilderness, motes of dust in a vast sky.

The driver of the lorry showed me the place where he had pulled off the highway and had first discovered the tragedy. In the hope that Judy might have been afraid to leap from the moving vehicle and had jumped down when he came to a stop, I searched the area meticulously for tracks. I made circles, ever-increasing in diameter, looking in the dust of every goat or cattle trail. In an hour I was convinced that she had not left the lorry there.

At dusk we met at Lion Camp and discussed the situation. Several possibilities were put forward. Someone thought that Judy would have a homing instinct and, given time and luck, she would eventually return on her own to *Campi ya Simba*. Fortunately, her brother Francis, who was to have flown off with her that afternoon, was still with us as he had come back in his crate with the truck. If she did return in the middle of the night, Francis would be a solid magnet to hold her at Lion Camp.

Someone else thought that we should notify the owners of the large farms in the area where she had disappeared. This we did immediately. We also advised the Game Department in case a wandering lion cub was reported. The use of a spotting plane or helicopter was suggested and rejected. Chances of seeing that tawny lion in the grass from the air were too slim to be worth the effort. Better that we concentrate on more practical methods.

It was someone's idea that we might make the situation very public, offer a reward. This notion had delicate contingencies. Our concern might bring false claims of livestock or even people injured by a non-existent lion. A film company, with its association with millions of dollars, is particularly vulnerable to such shady accusations. Even though *information* would be the basis of the proposed reward, the most honest person might see our wayward cub and try to capture her himself – and end up by being seriously scratched or bitten. We decided not to advertise our potential liability.

The only positive conclusion we reached that night was that the cub might possibly return to the camp due to a homing instinct. In the meanwhile, we must search for her ourselves, quickly and diligently.

We thought that she could get along without food for about ten days. After that she would become too weak to travel. We knew that she was too young and inexperienced to hunt wild game and kill for herself. It was nearing the end of the dry season. In fact every afternoon now, banks of clouds threatened the beginning of the long rains, but there were many stock tanks and boreholes on the plains where Judy could find water. That aspect of her plight should not be a problem for her.

The following day we drove in shifts, one group searching in the morning, another group in the afternoon. At nightfall there was still no clue. The most discouraging thing was the vastness of the area which we had to search. If only we had a starting point; if only we knew where she had jumped off the truck. The time when we must leave Africa was growing close. Our job was really done, only our obligation to Judy kept us there. But for how long could we persist in this hopeless search?

The next day we walked, covering miles of plains and bush,

looking for the single track that would at least tell us the area on which to concentrate. I found the carcass of a steinbuck, freshly killed by some small predator, but there were no lion cub tracks in the area. It did however bring out one fact. If *I* could find a carcass, so could *Judy*. She might not be able to hunt and kill, but she could probably keep herself alive, barely, on carrion. It was a mixed blessing. It was reassuring that she might be able to survive for longer than the ten days we had originally given her – but would it only prolong her anguish and suffering as she slowly wasted away? And this made it impossible for us to put a limit on the time we could allow ourselves to search. How long does one look for a lost lion cub before giving up?

One aspect of this problem was in our favour. Sieuwke Bisleti, who was closest to Judy, would not be leaving. This area was her home, and even if Judy were not found and the rest of us must go away, Sieuwke would still be here to carry on.

A contractor showed up to begin dismantling *Campi ya Simba*. The producer sent him away. If the Lion Camp was to be a magnet to draw Judy back, it must remain untouched. In the event she was not found by the time of our final departure, arrangements were made for Sieuwke to stay on, the camp would be maintained, leases on search vehicles would be extended, and the maintenance staff would carry on.

Flight plans for Judy's brother Francis were cancelled because he could be a big help in retrieving her. Judy would always return to Francis, even if she were too frightened by her experiences to come to Sieuwke's call.

The next day Hubert, Sieuwke, Cheryl and I drove out again, stopping at clearings in the grass to check for tracks, looking in the trampled earth around watering places. We knew that Judy would lie up during the midday heat, hiding in some thick patch of bush, and if she were travelling it would only be during the cooler hours. In spite of the futility, we scanned far horizons with binoculars.

We asked herd boys, girls going for water, women gathering wood, anyone we saw, if they had seen a cub or lion tracks. 'Looking for a lost tame lion . . .?' Our query was regarded thoughtfully. We were eyed variously with suspicion, condescension, interest, fear. The reactions were as different as the people we questioned; but no one had seen a sign. We realized the similarities between our story and the real-life saga we had filmed of the Adamsons and their heartbreaking search for Elsa's cubs. On the fourth day of fruitless searching, we saw a shepherd with his flock on a wide rolling plain. A herd of zebras moved away from the Land-Rover as we approached him, and Thompson's gazelles grazed along the edge of the flock. He was a tall Masai, and Sieuwke, the only one of us who could speak the local language, opened the conversation in Swahili. I sat back and sighed. The words were incomprehensible to me. She didn't know the Masai language, which is a very different tribal tongue than the more widely used cross-tribal Swahili. Evidently there were only a few words and phrases of common understanding between Sieuwke and the shepherd. I could tell that Sieuwke was having difficulty making herself understood. But he was a friendly man and tried hard to comprehend.

At last he smiled broadly and pointed into the distance, emphasizing the farness with a clearly readable gesture. Several miles away in the direction he pointed, across the grasslands in the direction of the Nairobi Highway, a single scrubby tree stood silhouetted on the horizon. There was something affirmative in the Masai's attitude that registered to me even through the barrier of language.

'What's he saying?' I asked.

Sieuwke ignored my interruption and went on with the Swahili interrogation. Her Italian associations began to be revealed—gesticulations are a universally understood part of conversation.

'What's he saying?' I asked again.

'I don't think he understands me,' Sieuwke said. 'Or maybe I don't understand him. But I think he's telling us that he saw the tracks of a lion cub over by that tree.'

'When?' I asked her.

More incomprehensible words and gestures. At last: 'This morning. He'll show us.'

The tall Masai said something to a boy of about eight, who I gathered was to be left in charge of the sheep. Then he climbed into our crowded Land-Rover. The smoky-sweet smell of Masai cosmetics oozed into the car with him, slightly nauseating until one became used to it. The odour was said to have the benefit of inhibiting cattle flies, but evidently the flies that followed him into the car had long ago become immune.

Our experiences had already taught us that a ride in an automobile is an experience greatly cherished by Masai, and sometimes tribespeople used deceit to obtain a lift. But our new friend was obviously sincere. He went on, Sieuwke interpreting, proudly telling us of his skill as a tracker. With the disappointments of four days behind us, I remained to be convinced.

We arrived at the tree and he hopped out, smiling, pointing to a place on the trampled ground. Nothing but sheep tracks. Of course, he said, he couldn't actually show us the tracks here, his flock had passed over the area since he had seen them. We had asked him to show us where the tracks *had been*, and this was the place. Our disappointment registered. But this was only the *last* place he had seen the tracks, he continued. Up near the highway a mile away, he would show us lion tracks if that was what we wanted to see.

He stepped out of the Land-Rover beside the barbed-wire fence that paralleled the macadam road, squinting in several directions as if gathering his bearings. He walked straight to a gully that came from a culvert beneath the highway, stepped down the stock-path that ran along the fence and pointed at the ground with his *rungu* stick. There, vaguely, but without any doubt at all, was a lion track; not a full-grown lion's, but small, just the size of Judy's.

He pointed to a brushy hillside a couple of miles away on the other side of the highway. There was a concrete stock trough up there, he said, and he had heard about the lion from another man who had seen tracks by the trough the day before. He had gone there this morning to see for himself and had followed the tracks down the hill and across the road until he had lost them out on the plains by the tree. But the lion, he assured us, had drunk from the water tank on the last two consecutive nights.

That evening when we arrived at the water trough it was as the Masai had said. There were lion prints everywhere, coming and going, but always in the general direction of the place beside the highway where we had seen the track. We could look down from the trough and see the culvert, the lonely scrubby tree far out on the plain.

We reasoned that Judy had jumped from the lorry somewhere near the culvert, and she had returned here repeatedly, the only familiar spot in strange frightening surroundings. It was heart-breaking to think that while we had been looking for her, sometimes miles away, she had been searching for us, returning to that one known reference point, undoubtedly the location where she had leaped from the speeding lorry, the recognized place on the highway with its traffic of cars and trucks, the only familiar sights, sounds and odours, in this wild unknown land-scape.

That night we parked a van with built-in lion cage beside the water trough. It was the vehicle in which she often rode, and it was associated with many good experiences. Francis was inside, and in the empty space beside his cage we placed straw bedding and a chunk of fresh beef.

We hated to leave Francis there in the strange place in the middle of the African bush, all night long, alone. We knew he would be lonely and would call for company long into the night. It seemed a bit heartless as we drove away, but it was the best thing we could do for Judy. If Judy returned to the water trough, as she had the past two nights, she would hear Francis, and would go to him. Once beside her brother she would never leave the familiar van.

We were in high spirits that night, contemplating our day's success. Even if Judy failed to come back to the trough tonight, we had narrowed the area of our search from the thirty miles of highway and the vast wilderness we had been patrolling. We were closing in; surely it would not be long.

The next morning we parked a half-mile from the trough and walked the last distance so as not to frighten her away. We all had the highest optimism that she would be curled up on the straw beside her brother. He heard our approach, called his signal of recognition. She was not there. No tracks dimpled the fresh-raked ground. Last night she had not come to the area at all.

Sieuwke had brought with her the best-known bushman in the area, Ndengé, a professional gun-bearer and elephant tracker of the Wakamba tribe. He would accompany her on all future searches. Today, he found no fresh sign.

I spent two more fruitless days of searching and then I had to fly to London to begin editing the film. I should have left forty-eight hours earlier. Now at least I would leave satisfied that Sieuwke had everything she would need to carry on the search alone. The plan was that she would keep Francis until his sister was found, and then ship both together when Judy had recovered from her ordeal. She would have a search vehicle, a tracker, *Campi ya Simba* would be kept open, and she could draw whatever funds would be required. The producers were totally aware of their obligation and of our responsibility to Judy.

Judy's tracks had been reported at another watering place only a couple of miles from the trough on the hill. Sieuwke planned to sleep with Francis in the van near one waterhole, and at all the other watering places in the area she would place one of the cub's shelter houses from *Campi ya Simba*, each one with a bed of straw and with fresh meat. We thought that if Judy found one of these familiar houses, she would stay in it.

It was particularly frustrating to know that the cat was looking for us while we were looking for her, and that only very bad luck had kept our paths from crossing. If she found any familiar reminder of us, we felt sure that she would stay with it.

We were confident that luck would eventually bring our paths together. Our most disturbing apprehension was that the rains might come before we found her. If the long rains came, soaking the parched plains, Judy would no longer have need to visit the livestock watering troughs. Searching for us, she might wander away from the only fragile points of reference we had in common. Every day seemed as if it would be the last before the sky opened up. Farmers were begging for the water in the heavy clouds to fall, and we were praying for it to hold off just a little while longer.

When I left, Sieuwke was the last member of our company remaining to carry on the search, but she was surely the most qualified. It was a wearying, worrisome prospect but she faced the responsibility with positive resolution.

I was back in the London cutting rooms when I received the last sad news of Judy's end. Mercifully, neither Sieuwke nor Judy had to endure much more fear or hardship.

The good fortune which had followed us throughout the picture was not to return again now that, at the very end, our good luck had changed to bad. The final circumstances of Judy's death could not be more ill-fated by coincidence and the unexpected.

Judy's end, as well as it could be fitted together from bits and pieces of information filtered in from various sources, must have come more or less as Sieuwke worked it out and reported it to me.

The Lake Naivasha area is not one known in this day for its

wild lions. There is plenty of common plains game, antelope and other hooved animals, in the locality, but farming operations have made it unsuitable for wild lions. The areas to the south and west, however, do support wild prides, and occasionally a single lion or small family wanders through the Naivasha hills. It was by a rare coincidence, then, that at the very time that our Judy was loose on the country, a mother lioness and her four half-grown cubs were wandering north from Suswa and had entered these tracts of usually lionless plains.

While we were searching for Judy at the waterholes of Marula Farm, the mother lioness (unknown to us) was shot at another farm only ten miles from Judy's watering place, leaving her four cubs, like Judy, helpless wandering orphans.

On the very day we had searched fruitlessly for lion tracks to the west, these four cubs were seen by herders not far from Judy's area and heading in her direction. But this scrap of information, however useful or useless it might have been, we did not discover until after Judy's death.

Sieuwke thinks the four cubs, a desperate half-pride of wild lions, searching for water and food as Judy was, came into her territory and drove her out. In fact the influence of those cubs on the situation can never be known; one can only speculate on what occurred between them, and since all five cubs were definitely in the same area at the same time, it seems fairly certain that they must have met. Why four strange cubs would drive Judy away from the familiar area and the security of her watering places, we cannot guess. Surely that cooling water trough must have been a welcome discovery to the four cubs after crossing the arid plains, but would they in their frantic desperation drive another cub away?

All we know for sure is that before dawn on the morning of May 31st, on the very day I left for London, Judy entered the sheep corral of a farmer in the Mara Ngishu district, deep in the bush and hills, six miles away from her water trough and the familiar highway. Judy mauled four sheep and killed another before she was chased away by the night watchman. She returned at daylight and was shot through the eye from a distance of twenty feet as she crouched over the dead sheep, desperate, lonely, and afraid, defending her first and only kill.

Referring again to Sieuwke Bisleti's diary, I find this entry:

If she had been less independent, less self-sufficient, she might still be alive today. She might have tried to come back to camp instead of attempting to take care of herself.... It's funny, that the only outlined mark of a paw in my diary, of all the lions I ever had, should be Judy's.

Kwaheri
Means
Goodbye

Judy's death was an unhappy conclusion to our story in Africa, but we faced it realistically. The entire film experience, in spite of its final sadness, had been one of the most enjoyable and satisfying of my life. Since I was a child, I had wanted to visit East Africa and see its wildlife. But until I was actually there, I had no idea *how much* I had wanted to visit it, or how much I would have missed if I had not come.

Judy's end forced me to recall a phrase the naturalist Ernest Thompson Seton had written fifty years ago: 'There is only one way to make an animal's history untragic, and that is to stop before the last chapter.'

I wonder if the wild animals of Africa face a better fate?

There is considerable controversy today over the future of animals in East Africa, and nearly any afternoon in the shade of the Thorn Tree Café in Nairobi, at the corners of Kenyatta Avenue and Kimathi, one can hear the question discussed with objectivity, thoughtfulness, reason, and above all with emotion, from two directly opposite points of view.

To some stockmen, wild herds are only competitors for grass and water, and spreaders of disease. To some agriculturalists, land is fallow and useless until it is fenced and turned by a plough. Can any socially conscientious person, I have heard it asked, in a country increasingly populated by subsistence farmers, justify reserving huge tracts of land exclusively for animals?

Herds and man once lived in perfect equilibrium on the vast

savannah plains of East Africa, and the people who have lived
here since the dawn of man were as much part of the ecology as
the animals themselves. But now and ever increasingly so, the
balance has been disturbed. Or is it simply that the ecology of the
whole world is changing? Perhaps this seemingly unnatural thing
that is happening with the ascendancy of man as the earth's most
explosively reproducing animal is actually a part of the natural
evolution of our world. Maybe there is no place any more for
wild beasts. Perhaps they must go, along with open spaces and
quiet places. An upheaval that was felt a few years ago as a far off
tremor across the plains, has become an eruption, and people,
masses of them, are now flowing like molten lava from a
volcano, spreading out and consuming the land.

It seems obvious that land which is needed by human beings to
provide food and is occupied only by wild animals is land
wrongly used. But man has needs other than eating. Are the
other things that some men yearn for: wild landscapes, unclut-
tered shores, clean blue sky, nature, of any *real* value? Or are
they only embellishments to life, self-indulgences enjoyed by a
few? These are subtle things, values which cannot be declared in
bold decisive terms.

There is, I believe, a universal quality in man, an intuitive
desire for those basic values which he wants but which are so
difficult to express and define. The feeling is partly an emotion, a
painful yearning, acknowledged but not explained, a subtle
craving. There is emptiness without it, fulfilment with it . . . like
a love affair.

While I was in Africa I took a short safari to the Makindu
district, north of Hunter's Lodge. It was an area that had been
described to me as the best rhino country in East Africa, and I
hoped to get some shots for our film. This experience clarified
the problem for me. I rode out early in the morning on a
catching car with two friends, second generation of a family who
have captured wild game all over East Africa for export to zoos.

Once game-catching was a full adventuresome life. Now it is nearly finished as a profitable occupation, and in a few years these same men, along with the other ex-game-catchers, will probably be selling used cars or working at a job with a retirement pension plan just like anyone else.

I won't go into the excitement of those wild, crazy days of chasing rhinos at full speed through slashing thorns and over battering boulders – of the bruises, the scratches, the aches, and the exhilaration of what must be one of the world's most dangerous and active occupations. The significant thing about the exercise was not how we caught the rhinos, but *where* and *why* we did it. We drove in two battered catching cars and a pick-up lorry, in a wide-spaced formation through thickets of thorn left standing between small cleared plots and tin-roofed huts. A few months before, this had been pristine thorn bush and baobab forest. Now the area had been opened for settlement, and would-be agriculturalists were trying to eke subsistence from this inhospitably arid land.

Rhinos were browsing on the thorn fences of tiny farms, cut off by encroaching developments, living in islands of bush growing ever smaller as the perimeters were hacked away. Smoke from clearing fires rose in pale grey clouds, and the tsetse flies which had kept out humans and livestock for a thousand years, and which could not live except under the shelter of trees, attacked us with dying vigour.

My companions had been given permits for as many rhinos as they could capture in Makindu. The animals were doomed anyway, and it was the only way to salvage some from the poisoned arrows of the newly arrived African settlers. Of the nearly thirty rhinos we caught in the area, all but three of the smallest babies had festering arrow or spear wounds. Rhino carcasses lay scattered through the bush, under the trees where hidden archers had fired their lethal poison.

It is an old story, often told, from all over the world: farmers and wild animals cannot live side-by-side. The real threat to the wildlife of Africa is not from poachers or hunters, from cropping or from not cropping; it is from the constant encroachment on the wilderness by people anxious to turn the land into something it has never been before. Population is the disease, development the sickness. The other things are only symptoms.

One opinion discussed over those tables at the Thorn Tree Café is that when pressures for the land become greater, the large parks will have to go; that except for a few small fenced-off plots that will really be nothing more than zoos, people will ultimately kill off the last of the animals.

Others say that as long as tourists come here from other parts of the world to see the animals, and the land has value because of the money it brings, the tracts will continue to be held aside for game.

The argument goes on, and the animals continue to decline.

For me, the animals and the countryside of East Africa have been the great experience of my life. The thought of those wide plains cluttered with tin roofs and riven with impenetrable fences is repulsive. A great deal more would be gone for me, than only the animals. It would be an emotional thing I would be missing, something of what makes life worth living, perhaps in a different way a need as vital as food itself, subtle, difficult to define . . . like a love affair.

Acknowledgements

I wish to thank the following:

ACHUGA (Driver), George ADAMSON (Source Material), Joy ADAMSON (Source Material), Taj and Taboo AHAMED (Costumes), Stuart ALLISON (Stunt Driver), ANNA (Caterer), Jim ASH (Lion Country Safari), John AYTON (Freight), Cesar AZAVEDO (Freight), Alan BALLARD (Special Still Photographer), Sid BARNSBY (Production Supervisor), John BAXENDALE (Safari Manager), Robert BEAUMONT (Cast), David BEGG (Locations), Cesare and Pappa BERINGHERI (Locations), Susie BIRTWISTLE (Nurse), Sieuwke BISLETI (Animal Handler), Jack and E. R. BLOCK (Locations), Norman BOLLAND (Location Sound Mixer), Dr Reginald BUNNY (Company Doctor), Margaret BURKE (Catering), Heather CAMPBELL (Veterinary), Jill CARPENTER (Make-Up), Carl, Roy and Brian CARR-HARTLEY (Wildlife), Sarah CHILD (Stand-In), Sheila COLLINS (London Liaison), John COX (Sound Supervisor), John CRAWFORD (Focus-Puller), Nigel DAVENPORT (Cast), Don DEACON (Editor), Shane DE LOUVRE (Cast), Mohinder DHILLON (Publicity Photography), Bill DREDGE (Lion Country Safari), Martin DUNFORD (Catering), Graham DUNCANSON (Veterinary), Dave EDWARDS (Transport), Desmond EDWARDS (Sound Maintenance), Hal FISHER (Transport), Carl FOREMAN (Executive Producer), CABRIEL (Driver), GEOFFREY (Driver), Jackson GITHOI (Driver), Samuel GITONGA (Carpenter), Andy GRAY (Grip), Marion GRAY (Publicity Secretary), Ken GREEN (Publicity), Chris GREENHAM (Dubbing Editor), Terry GREENWOOD (Propman), John HALL (Laboratory Contact), George HAMILTON (Spark), HAMISI (Driver), Susan HAMPSHIRE (Cast), Norman HARGOOD (Still Photographer), Tony and Susan HARTHOORN (Veterinary), Charles HAYES (Accommodations and Cast), Jean HAYES (Cast), Mike HAYES (Catering), HASSAN (Kenya National Parks), Ralph HELFER (Lions), Mike HIGGINS (Locations), Rozz HILLYAR (Secretary), Noreen HIP-WELL (Production Secretary), Pat HOWELL (Accountant), Samson HUTI (Driver), Big JOHN (Catering), Edward JUDD (Cast), Maulishi JUMA (Spark/Standby), Stanley KAHAGI (Driver), James KAMAU (Cast), Saul KAPLAN (Composer), Millard KAUFMAN (Screenplay), Cricket KENDALL (Publicity), David KERR (Lion Food), Derek KINGSMILL (Assistant Editor), Musagar KIPENGWA (Campi ya Simba), Geoffrey ole KUSERU (Game Department), Raman LADD (Transport), Neil LARK-

MAN (Insurance), Philip LEAKEY (Safaris), Dave LEONARD (Pilot, Safari Air Services), Joe LEONARD (Freight), Philip LEWIS (Camera Equipment Contact), Tony LEWIS (Laboratory Contact), Peter LUKOYE (Cast), Joseph LUCAS (Driver), Ronnie MAASZ (Camera Operator), George MACHARIA (Driver), G. N. MACHARIA (Game Department), Peter MAGIUS (Local Assistant), Viscount Kim MANDEVILLE (Stunt Driver), MARIKO (Office Helper), Angela MARTELLI (Continuity), MARY (Catering), Willem van MASTRIOT (Communications), Mutua MATUA (Driver), Lional MILLS (Insurance), Eva MONLEY (Production Manager), Jeff MOYES (Gaffer), Mr MUTINDA (Game Department), Mr MWANIKI (District Officer, Naivasha), MWANIKO (Driver), Dr Andreas von NAGY (Wildlife), David NDEGWA (Local Assistant Director), Samson NDISII (Driver), Peter NDUNGU (Driver), Joseph NGALANGE (Driver), Ivo NIGHTINGALE (Assistant Director), Col. John NIMMO (Locations), John NJENGA NYORO (Campi ya Simba), Nobby NOBLE (Cast), Stephen NYAGA (Carpenter), Mr NYANGAO (Postmaster, Naivasha), John OWEN (Tanzania National Parks), Perez OLINDO (Kenya National Parks), PATRICK (Catering), PETER (Catering), Aludin QUERSHI (Cast), Paul RADIN (Producer), Jenny RICHARDSON (Office), Mike RICHMOND (Kenya Equipment), Willy ROBERTS (Animal Handler), Don ROMNEY (Distributors' Representative), RUBANGA (Driver), Jackie RUBEN (Transport), Monty RUBEN (Liaison), George RUGERO (Transport), Staff of R.S.P.C.A. (Lion care, London Airport), SAFARI Staff (Philip Leakey Safaris), John SAMWORTH (Sound Technician), Emperor HAILE SELASSIE (who provided 5 lions), Cheryl SHAWVER (Animal Handler), Jon SHEPHARD (Freight), Harry SHUSTER (Lion Country Safari), Michael SLOAN (Assistant Editor), John STAHNKE (Stand-In), John STOLL (Art Director), Wolfgang SUSCHITZKY (Director of Photography), Abdulla SUNADO (Props), TAISWA (Masai Foreman), Peter TERRY (Assistant Dubbing Editor), Nigel THOMPSON (East Africa Airways), Dick THOMSETT (Publicity Photography), P. THORPE (Locations), Julian TONGUE (National Parks), Annie TREGARTHEN (Transport), Michael TUCKER (Soundboom Operator), Myles TURNER (Tanzania National Parks), Paul WELD DIXON (Publicity Photography), Hubert WELLS (Head Animal Handler), John WILLIS (Publicity), Eileen WOOD (Executive Producer's Secretary), Bill WOODLEY (Kenya National Parks), David WYNN-JONES (Clapper-Loader), Dave WYATT (Travel), Bill YORK (Lion Country Safari).